Frank Topping was born into a Catholic family on the Wirral peninsula in 1937. He left his school, St Anselm's College, Birkenhead, at 15 because of family illness, but went back to complete his O levels when the family improved. As a boy he played the cornet in the Birkenhead Borough Silver Prize Band and was second cellist in the school orchestra.

His ear for dialects and his love of poetry won him a scholarship to the North West School of Speech and Drama.

After National Service in the Middle East during the EOKA troubles and the Suez crisis, he returned to England to become stage-manager/electrician and assistant carpenter with the Leatherhead Repertory Company, where he also played minor roles. At this time he met and married June, a Methodist, who had joined the Repertory Company.

Whilst working in other theatres and in television, Frank, who had lost his faith years before, began to study theology under the guidance of the Reverend Derrick Greeves, who was the Methodist minister at Westminster Central Hall. In 1964 he became a theological student at Bristol and in 1970 was ordained a Methodist minister. As a probationer he served at the famous Dome Mission in Brighton and as a Methodist chaplain to Sussex University.

His offer _____ with the religious programmes at BBC Radio Brigh _____ his becoming Assistant Religious _____ BBC North Region in _____ n, editor of a variety of r _____ For The Day' and 'Paus _____ for mimicry, music and _____ le of religious broadcasting. He has writt _____ d a number of devotional books. He is now known to millions for his radio and TV programmes and not least for his partnership with Donald Swann which led to the West End production of 'Swann with Topping'.

Frank and June have three children and live in North Wales.

To the
Reverend Dr Frederick Greeves
with gratitude

FRANK TOPPING

God Bless You —
Spoonbill

Letters to a young minister

Drawings by
Zena Flax

Collins
FOUNT PAPERBACKS

First published by Fount Paperbacks, London in 1984

© Frank Topping, 1984

Copyright in the drawings
© William Collins Sons & Co Ltd, 1984

Made and printed in Great Britain by
William Collins Sons & Co Ltd, Glasgow

Introduction

There are at least two ways of tackling a problem. You can, as it were, strike immediately, grab it by the scruff of the neck as a hawk that drops like a stone on its prey; or you might, as I am inclined, glide in lazy circles, like a gull considering its quarry from a distance, preoccupied and easily distracted from the final swoop.

Some time ago, whilst circling the problem of how to set about writing a book of pastoral theology, I was distracted by a description of an exotic African bird called a 'Spoonbill'. Apart from the shape of its beak an extraordinary feature of its character is its silence. It has never been heard to emit a sound other than a grunt, and that only in the mating season. Allowing these odd facts to distract me further I doodled the following rhyme.

> The Spoonbill is a quiet bird
> quite silent in the hunt,
> save in the mating season, when,
> he has been heard to grunt.
> Although we never hear
> the voice he hasn't got,
> whilst gazing down his spoon-shaped bill
> I think he thinks a lot.

Many an ecclesiastical synod member is given to doodling, either rhymes about, or sketches of, his synod brethren. At this particular time I was not at synod but on the Norfolk Broads. My doodle took on a life of its own. Quite suddenly and almost complete in every detail the Reverend Walter Spoonbill entered my mind; a quiet thinker, a parson of long experience, kindly and wise, a friend of the lonely with comfort for the suffering and encouragement for the young. He was the answer to my pastoral theology problem. The Reverend Walter Spoonbill would be the man to turn to for advice and scholarship.

In no time at all, or so it seemed, I discovered his tutorial relationship with the young ordinand, Tommy Sefton-Waters. Tommy marched into my head bringing with him students, farmers, estate managers, husbands, wives, sinners and sinned against. He also introduced me to a countryside, a valley, the Woodley Vale, complete with rivers, market towns, villages and farms.

He made it abundantly clear that pastoral theology is not something you read but something you do. It is a way of life informed by prayer and faith. It is an attempt to follow, however imperfectly, in the footsteps of Christ.

What has emerged is a theological exercise, but it is also the story of a young man's attempts to come to terms with his faith and his call to the ministry.

Preface

I first met the Reverend Thomas Sefton-Waters during a boating holiday on the Norfolk Broads. I was not strictly on holiday. October is rather out of season for Broads boating. I was actually in retreat in order to finish writing a book. An out-of-season Broads boat is the ideal place to escape from the telephone, the postman, the doorbell and the great variety of interruptions that can be either a source of irritation, or at best an opportunity to exercise patience.

I had made my way from Wroxham to Horning, intending to book a table at The Swan for my evening meal. One of the difficulties of single-handed boating is that when coming alongside a bank, a vessel needs to be secured fore and aft, so if there is a willing bystander who will take the bow-line whilst you deal with the stern, the solo boatsman is only too grateful.

Approaching the waterside lawns of The Swan I was relieved to see the figure of a robust, white-haired old man not only marching towards the bank but calling to me 'Right oh, old chap, let's have your bow-line!'

So many important events in our lives seem to depend on chance or accident. I little realized at the time that this particular chance meeting would be the beginning of a friendship that was to last for many years.

We dined together that night at The Swan and I learned that he was a retired Methodist minister who had served his church in places as distant and different as India and the Virgin Islands. Tommy Sefton-Waters was a jolly, kindly and competent man. He could weld a storm-roof on a tin chapel, extract teeth or discuss hermeneutics. For forty years he had preached, visited and advised; baptized, married and committed to the hereafter – always accompanied by his wife Sally, who had died a few years before I met him. He had talked, laughed and listened in some of the most outlandish and unlikely places on earth. For a writer, meeting him was like finding gold.

His little house in Horning became a place of pilgrimage for me every year until he died. It was in the year that he died that he introduced me to Spoonbill, or rather, the Reverend Walter Spoonbill.

Spoonbill had been dead for a good number of years, so naturally I did not meet him face to face, but the curious thing was that Tommy Sefton-Waters had never met him face to face either, despite the fact that for three years Spoonbill had been Tommy's personal tutor.

When Tommy had left his college, in the early thirties, he had been appointed to a rural circuit in Herefordshire. He was then what Methodists call a probationer, that is, an ordinand given limited authority to minister in a circuit prior to ordination. The probationary period usually lasts about three years, and during this time the ordinand continues his studies under the guidance of a personal tutor – an experienced minister living in a different circuit. The probationer is required to visit his tutor regularly, write essays for him, discuss his book list with him and confide in him as his spiritual director. Living in a different circuit enables the ordinand to discuss pastoral and personal problems with someone who is completely indifferent and impartial.

In his first few months as an ordinand, Tommy found it impossible to settle on mutually convenient days to meet his tutor. Letters passed to and fro until Spoonbill suggested that perhaps, in order to get started, it would help if Tommy sent him a weekly account of his work and he, Spoonbill, would make notes and reply in the following week. Whilst not being totally satisfactory, it would enable them to get acquainted on paper until the happy day when both their diaries allowed them to meet.

Habits are easy to form, but difficult to break. For three years Tommy wrote his weekly account and for three years Spoonbill replied to him and sent satisfactory reports to the church's ministerial training department. Illness prevented Spoonbill from attending Tommy's ordination, and immediately after his ordination Tommy left for the Virgin Islands. So, they never met. Later Spoonbill sent all of Tommy's original letters to the Virgin isles, believing, quite rightly, that Tommy might like them as an account of his first three years in the ministry.

One October evening, sitting in Tommy Sefton-

Waters' study, I was shown the Spoonbill correspondence. He had treasured the letters all his ministry. Whether or not Tommy had a premonition of his death, I don't know, but as I was leaving he gave me the three bulging folders that had accompanied him around the world. 'Take them,' he said, 'I'm sure you will find them interesting. I don't need them now. I practically know everything that Spoonbill wrote by heart. Whenever I faced a decision I always asked myself, "What would Spoonbill have said?"' Tommy smiled. 'Of course he doesn't have all the answers to everything, but he always provided a good jumping off ground.'

I protested that they were surely too precious to give away, but Tommy said, 'Not at all; anyway, it won't be long now before Spoonbill and I finally meet up with one another.'

That was the last time I saw Tommy Sefton-Waters. He died in his sleep two months later, on Christmas Eve.

To reproduce the entire three-year exchange of letters would, I fear, involve several volumes. Therefore for this book I have chosen a cross-section of extracts from the Sefton-Waters-Spoonbill files and edited them.

Listening to the water lapping against my boat, the *Water Gypsy*, I know that Tommy would not mind my sharing his Spoonbill letters with anybody who might benefit from them; perhaps that is why he gave them to me. I am equally sure that Spoonbill would not mind either.

F.T., Norfolk Broads, 1983

The First Year

**The Manse,
Norton Woodley**

Dear Mr Spoonbill,

Thank you for the suggestion of sending a weekly account of day-to-day notes. I think it's a very good idea. It should, at the very least, introduce some discipline into my life. I think perhaps I had better start with a survey of my first few weeks as a probationary minister. So many things have happened in such a short space of time, putting my impressions on to paper might help me to sort out the confusion.

My arrival in Norton Woodley at the end of August was a far more exciting experience than I had expected. The superintendent minister had written to say that he would meet me at the Norton Woodley manse at 11 a.m. on Wednesday, the 21st August. I had imagined that he would shake hands, give me the key to the front door, together with his blessing, and that, more or less, would be that. I certainly didn't expect to find a house full of people and activity and a larder piled high with food.

The chapel stewards were there with their wives, John Fielding, his wife Hetty, and 'Dusty' Baker with his wife Monica. Both of them are farming families. Dusty has a slightly clownish appearance and, I suspect, a clownish humour to match. He is short and solid. His face is burned red from years of working in the fields, red that is up to the line of his cap, from there to his sandy hair his forehead is lily white. Monica, his wife, has a similar rotundity and the same huge smile.

John Fielding, who Dusty constantly referred to as 'Long John', is as different from Dusty as it is possible to be. He is tall and almost painfully thin. I don't think he is weak, it is a kind of stringy, sinewy leanness. He has the most extraordinary bushy black eyebrows, made all the more outstanding by the fact that his hair is absolutely white. I don't think I saw him smile once; however, the superintendent assures me that he is a good man, totally devoted to the chapel. His wife, Hetty, is a frail-looking woman. She does smile, nervously. I noticed that whenever she smiled she glanced quickly at her husband as if seeking his approval.

I was introduced to Mrs McBride and learned to my utter bewilderment that she is to be my housekeeper. She is the widow of a Scotsman who spent most of his days farming in Wales. When he died, Mrs McBride decided to return to her home village in the Woodley Vale. She speaks with words and phrases borrowed from her Scottish husband and her years on a Welsh farm, without having lost any of her Herefordshire country burr. I remember looking at her sharply to see if she was joking when she said,

'Mrs Baker brought that wee posy of flowers on the table, now there's lovely, isn't it?' I'm sure she's not aware of the hybrid nature of her speech.

The superintendent's wife, Mrs Frobisher, seems shrewd, humorous and quiet, whereas the Reverend Mr Frobisher is as noisy and hearty a man as I have ever met. Nevertheless I'm convinced that behind the booming voice and the cherubic smile there lies a great deal of his wife's shrewdness.

Miss Fletcher, the Sunday school teacher, brought home-made shortbread. Henry Trevenna, who is Dusty's cowman, brought seedlings for the garden together with much 'knowing' advice with regard to nurturing them. Mrs Fielding produced a hand-embroidered table napkin, quite beautifully and painstakingly worked. Everybody, it seems, brought something for the larder. I ought to add that it was the superintendent who brought Mrs McBride. As I mentioned earlier, when he introduced her to me as my housekeeper I was quite shocked and not a little worried. I couldn't see how I could afford to pay her from a probationer's stipend. Later Mr Frobisher took me to one side and in a huge stage whisper told me not to worry, because, '. . . arrangements have been made, dear boy. Mrs McBride's wages need never concern you. You will find her a tower of strength. Mrs Frobisher's idea really, thinks you young ordinands need lookin' after.' He clearly did not intend to enlighten me further; perhaps I shall never know exactly where her wages come from. What little information he did give me was accompanied by encouraging pats on the shoulder and huge winks. Mrs McBride doesn't 'live in'. She has her own cottage, which happens to be next door to the Norton Woodley Methodist Church and next door but one to the manse.

The official welcome had been arranged for Saturday afternoon. It took the form of a service in the chapel followed by 'the welcome tea' in the school room. It was, I thought, a rather splendid service. People came from all the villages and the church was packed. There were five ministers including myself. Mr Frobisher conducted the service, a retired minister, Mr Barnes of Newton St Michael, read a lesson, and the vicar of Norton Woodley, Mr Allerton, also read a lesson. Mr Langley, who is semi-retired, and is the active supernumerary minister at Oakham, gave a welcoming address and also the 'charge to a new minister'. I was required to respond to his address and almost finished my ministerial life before it had begun.

On Friday Mr Frobisher had called at the manse to discuss the service; as he was leaving he said, 'Do you have a cassock and gown, dear boy?' I said, 'Yes, though I've never actually worn the cassock, my parents bought it for me only a few weeks ago.' Mr Frobisher beamed and said, 'Well then, it's cassock and gown on Saturday. You may never need to be so formal again in this circuit, but it will reassure the church members that they have a "proper" minister.'

It was the cassock that was nearly my undoing. There is a raised wooden pulpit in the Norton Woodley chapel. The pulpit is entered by means of a semi-circular staircase of six steps. As I ascended these steps, my mind on higher things, I made a classic mistake. I began to walk up the inside of my cassock. The result was that I crashed headlong into the pulpit. There was a gasp from the congregation, followed by a sigh of relief as their red-faced minister scrambled to his feet. I found myself saying, 'If pride goes before a fall, it certainly doesn't follow it.' The people laughed and the ice was broken, for what had been a rather solemn and formal service took on a new spirit. During the hymn that followed there were lots of smiles and exchanges of sidelong glances.

I'm not sure how long the welcoming continues, but so far I have been 'welcomed' in every chapel in the Woodley Vale, Oakham and Grayleton circuit, and at every church meeting and committee, since I arrived; and I have not yet visited every chapel.

I'm trying very hard to commit names and faces to memory, but it's very difficult. Sometimes I lie in bed trying to do a round of the farms and chapels in my head. I rarely get through the names of one family before sleep takes me. I suppose it's appropriate for a pastor to go to sleep counting his pastorate.

A strange thing happened in my second week at the manse. The manse, incidentally, is far too big for a bachelor. It is a rambling old house, mainly Victorian, with a huge garden. Not that I'm complaining, I like it very much. Well, on Thursday in my second week, Mrs Driver called at the manse with an extraordinary request. Her husband, Harold, had asked for me. They live at the bakery in the High Street, which they used to run together until Harold's illness. I visited them in my first week and learned that Harold had been ill for a very long time. His illness caused him a great deal of pain and he didn't look as if he was likely to recover. On that Thursday morning Harold asked his wife to request me to 'lay hands' on him and to pray that he would begin to get better or that he would be released from his pain. Shortly after giving these instructions he became comatose. Mrs Driver sent for the doctor who said that nothing could be done. She then came to me. I was in a quandary. I do not have, as far as I know, any gift for healing. I didn't want to raise false hopes and said as much to Mrs Driver. On the other hand I couldn't see any harm in carrying out his request. So I accompanied Mrs Driver to the bakery.

Harold looked dreadful. His eyes and face seemed to have sunk far more than when I had seen him earlier. At first I wondered if he was alive, but as I drew closer to him I could see that he was breathing. I asked Mrs Driver to join me in prayer. After we had prayed I placed my hands on Harold's chest and prayed the prayer he had requested.

When we had left the room I told Mrs Driver that I would be at home for the rest of the day should she need me. About ten minutes later, just as I was opening the door of the manse, my telephone started to ring. Harold had died almost as soon as I had left the bakery.

Mrs Driver is convinced that through me Harold's prayer was answered. She is convinced that I have a special spiritual gift. I have tried to persuade her that the timing of Harold's death was probably coincidental with my having just laid hands on him. I told her that the Almighty knew what Harold's prayer was without my saying it, and that Harold may well have died at that time, simply because that was the end of his struggle. She will not be persuaded. She smiles sadly at my protests, evidently seeing them as an expression of modesty or humility. I am no longer certain that I did the right thing. I fear I may have created a false impression of my spirituality in the mind of Mrs Driver, and I can see no way of undoing what has happened.

I must stop now. I didn't really intend to write so much. It's been a strange two weeks. I started paddling in the shallow end of the welcoming receptions and suddenly I have plunged into deep water. I'm not sure that I'm not already out of my depth!

With my best regards,

Thomas Sefton-Waters

My dear Thomas,

Thank you for your fascinating letter. Please do not apologize for its length. I enjoyed every word. I want you to write as you are able and as you feel. If you feel expansive, then so be it. If the pressure of work and time is such that you can only manage a few terse notes, they will be equally acceptable.

You have a good eye for detail, which is a useful skill that should be part of every minister's armoury. People often tell us far more about themselves with their hands, feet, eyes, smiles, sighs and hesitations, than they ever do in words. So much pastoral work is dependent on the minister being sensitive to moods and atmospheres, and being able to read accurately between the lines. Naturally, it requires a genuine interest in and concern for people – perhaps 'love' is a better word than 'concern'.

A minister should always listen more than he speaks. He should develop the ability to encourage people to talk. He should build relationships in which people feel relaxed in his company and therefore able to share whatever is on their minds. Unfortunately it is very easy to succumb to the temptation to talk in platitudes and clichés, and to burden people with shortened versions of old sermons as a substitute for conversation. Having spewed a torrent of parsonic words all over someone's kitchen or parlour, we might leave feeling tolerably pleased that we have fulfilled our pastoral duty whilst being totally unaware that behind the 'Yes, minister . . . no, minister' politeness lay a concealed anguish whose release we have successfully prevented.

Whilst we must give people the opportunity to speak, we should not be afraid of silence. In fact we should make it a practice to take a cup of tea without speaking more than is absolutely necessary. Short periods of shared silence can be enjoyed; they do not have to be embarrassing, nor are they when they provide people with the thinking time and the opportunity to express their concerns. By the use of short 'thought' prayers, even if nothing is said by either party, silence can be a simple way of sharing something of the peace of God. If this is the only thing that you are able to take into people's homes on your pastoral rounds, 'something of the peace of God', then your visits will not have been in vain.

We must be careful that these silences are genuinely prayer-filled moments. We must have no truck with pretend piety, mock modesty, or a 'show' of pastoral humility. Such pretence fools nobody except the pretender. It is really a question of taking one's mind entirely away from 'self' and concentrating instead on the person you are with. All of which is easier said than done.

I was very interested in your story about the 'laying on of hands' and Mr Driver's death. I am sure that you are right and that his death and your 'laying on of hands' was entirely coincidental. There is another possibility. I believe that one can never be certain of the exact state of consciousness of a person in a comatose condition. He might be incapable of movement, or speech, or even the least sign of being aware of what is going on around him. This does not mean that he is necessarily incapable of recognizing touch or hearing speech. If he had been able to hear you, you may have assisted his release. You may, through your prayer, have given him permission to relax his tenuous hold on life. You may have performed, in a simplified way, a form of what our Catholic brethren would call Extreme Unction. I think your response to the situation was perfectly proper, Christian and humane. You did what you believed to be the most loving thing to do. 'The most loving thing to do' is not a bad criterion to use when making these decisions, allowing that 'the most loving thing' may not always be the gentlest thing to do, or the most popular. With children, for instance, the most loving thing to do might be to protect them from something which would harm them, even though to them that 'something' may seem at that moment to be their heart's desire.

You must tell me more about Mrs Driver as time goes by. Sorrow and grief affect people in different ways. She may at this time be feeling relief and gratitude that her husband is no longer in pain. You say that Mr Driver had been ill for a long time, which means that for Mrs Driver all her time and activity was centred around her husband. It is quite likely that very shortly she will feel there is a great vacuum in her life. She will miss him. She may lose the sense of purpose in her life. She may feel cast adrift in a sea of loneliness. We must see what we can do to help her.

For the immediate present you must offer all the practical help you can. She may have family or friends who will be able to do these things, but if not, you must try to relieve her of the tedium of filling in forms, arranging insurance papers or any other administrative chore which someone in her condition will find difficult, if not impossible to concentrate on. Apart from any specific wishes she may have about the funeral arrangements she should be relieved of all other responsibilities, unless she is the kind of person who is able to use these tasks to keep her going.

Visit her and make yourself more than usually available to her. I am sure that you've done all these things, or are doing them. Forgive me for stating the obvious, but the obvious things can very easily be overlooked.

Give her the opportunity to talk. Sometimes people need to reminisce, to remember old times. She may want to ask questions about life and death, or life after death. She will not want a sermon, she may not be able to concentrate on anything you say, but she may need reassurance, simply expressed, about the things she already believes. You must give her that reassurance by expressing your own faith in the promises of Christ.

Perhaps it would be useful if you were to jot down some of your own thoughts about what scripture and the church teaches with regard to death and life after death, and your interpretation of those teachings.

Keep up the good work!

Yours sincerely,

Walter Spoonbill

Dear Mr Spoonbill,

On Saturday evening my sermon preparation was somewhat interrupted by the arrival of Miss Fletcher, Rene Fletcher, the Sunday school teacher, who was, commendably, anxious that her lessons with the children should complement whatever 'course' of sermons I might embark on. She put me to shame. My 'forward planning' is practically non-existent. She is a marvellous old girl. Perhaps I shouldn't call her old; she retired two years ago having spent nearly twenty years as secretary, and personal assistant to Fletcher & Swanley, our local solicitors. Her father was George Fletcher, who died about five years ago. She isn't qualified to do anything in particular. I think she simply helped her father, but I doubt if there is anything she doesn't know about local legal matters. She is a mine of information about absolutely everybody in Norton Woodley, from grandparents to grandchildren. We went through her Sunday school class lists. There are three classes: infants, juniors and seniors, with about fifteen to twenty children in each class. She knew the background of every child – what their parents did for a living, their personal problems and their temperaments.

I think she must be about sixty, though she doesn't look it. She is slim and neat. Her hair, which has very little grey in it, is swept back into a bun. She is very precise and reasonable, in fact she looks frighteningly efficient, except that her mouth betrays a sense of humour that she must struggle to control. It was a fascinating evening, even if I did get to bed rather late – very late. I think I finished working on my sermon about 2 a.m.

On Sunday morning I preached on the text, 'Behold the Lamb of God who takes away the sins of the world' (John 1:29). The theme was atonement. Here is a brief outline:

1. Biblical and historical evidence of man's inability to reconcile himself to God, to 'save himself'.

2. God so loved the world that, in spite of man's sinfulness, he gave his only begotten Son, 'The Lamb of God', to bear, to carry, the sin of the world. Sin crucifies love – but love cannot die – God is love, love conquers.

3. His victory – our victory. Christ is like the captain of a cricket team whose brilliant performance secures victory for a very weak team. The team, following their captain, leave the field victors in spite of all their failings.

After the service Roger Gumley, a local young farmer, said that he was interested in the sermon but found it difficult to see how somebody dying a few thousand years ago had anything to do with him. He wanted to see it, but just couldn't. I promised I would talk with him about it next time I was at Woodley

Bottom Farm. I think it is the problem of understanding our being limited by time, and God being outside of time. It's a difficult concept to put into plain words, but I suppose I'll have to try.

Every good wish,

Yours,

Thomas Sefton-Waters

The Manse,
Nether Hadley

Dear Thomas,

Your Sunday school teacher, Miss Fletcher, sounds extremely interesting and an absolute godsend to a minister new to the district.

It does sound as if you could benefit from some of her efficiency. I have to say this with my tongue in my cheek, God forgive me, because it is a case of the pot calling the kettle. However, you really must try to get a good night's sleep. Nobody functions well when they are short of sleep and preachers are no exception. There, it was my duty to say that and I've said it. Now to your sermon.

I appreciate your courage in tackling such a major theme. As you know, the classical theories of atonement are all flawed and imperfect in some way. This is hardly surprising considering that what is being attempted is a definition of the nature of God and the nature of God in Christ. It is somewhat ambitious to hope that we could even approach an explanation of the mind, purpose and method of Almighty God. But perhaps that is what makes man interesting, the fact that he thinks that he ought to be able to find a rational explanation for absolutely everything.

Acknowledging our universal and unsurprising failure to encompass the mind of God, nevertheless, on the question of God existing outside of time, there is an illustration which you may or may not find useful. When you next visit your young farmer, invite him to imagine that he is a great artist, a painter. Invite him to imagine that he is about to paint the greatest landscape that has ever been conceived, a picture of 'time', from the beginning to the end.

In order to conceive the vastness of this enterprise, invite him to imagine that he is standing on a beach at the seaside. He is looking at the great expanse of sea where it meets the horizon, and beyond that is an endlessly clear sky. As far as he can see, the sea and the sky is completely empty. That is his canvas.

Now let us begin to sketch in the picture. Starting far away to the left, we begin to paint. Darkness, the beginning of time. Then there is light, and mountains and lakes; creatures, fish and man, Adam and Eve, Abraham and Sarah, Moses, Joshua, Samson, prophets, all the people who ever lived, kings and princes, Greeks and Romans. As we move along the horizon we come to a figure on a cross, and then we see Paul, Augustine, emperors and popes, monasteries and monks, the crusades, St Francis of Assisi, Luther, Calvin, Quakers, Baptists, Cranmer, Anglicans, Wesley and the Methodists. On and on we move, sketching in all the secular world until this present day, politicians, prime ministers and presidents, doctors, lawyers, wives and mothers, you and me, our children, through wars and peace to children as yet unborn, beyond our present time to new ways of life, new forms of travel, unimagined buildings, towns and cities. On and on until the end of time.

We are on this picture and being on it we cannot see the whole of the work. But if we could step off the picture, if we could step out of time, if we could stand alongside the artist, we would be able to look at this great canvas and our eyes would be drawn to the man on the cross, Jesus Christ our Lord, who is dying for the sins of a Roman soldier thrusting a lance in his side. But he is dying not only for the sins of that soldier, but for the sins of Adam and Eve, Moses and David, Paul, Augustine, you and me, and our children, born and unborn, for the whole of mankind.

If you could stand alongside the painter of this great masterpiece, you would see everything in a single glance. You would see all of time in a single moment, you would see that Christ's sacrifice embraces all humanity, all creation from the beginning to the end.

Well, as I said, none of us are capable of entering into the mind of God but the attempt is always breathtakingly exciting!

Keep up the struggle; even if your young farmer cannot envisage the picture he will appreciate your effort. By the way, how is Mrs Driver? Thinking of her reminds me, I really would be interested to hear your thoughts on bereavement.

Yours ever,

Spoonbill

The Manse,
Norton Woodley

Dear Mr Spoonbill,

I simply must tell you about the Harvest Festival service at Woodley Park Chapel. It was a strange mixture of good fellowship and comic disaster, and certainly an experience I shall remember for many years to come.

Woodley Park is a tiny hamlet on the Grayleton Road. It is surrounded by farms, and the farming families are 'chapel' to a man, with the notable exception of the Honorable Richard Grey of Woodley Grange Farm. The Hon. Mr Grey, nevertheless, always attends the chapel Harvest Festival with his wife, Constance. He owns most of the land west of the Leaze, or rather his father, Lord Woodley, does.

The old man, who is eighty-nine, rarely puts a foot out of Grayleton Towers these days, except on high days and holidays. In Woodley Vale the Park Chapel Harvest Festival is undoubtedly a 'high' day.

I knew that the chapel was being 'dressed' for the occasion. Whenever I called at one of the farms during the preceding week, the 'missus' was always out, 'gettin' the chapel spruced up'. I stopped by the chapel once and was 'shooed' away by what seemed like a brigade of farmers' wives. I did get a glimpse of hop sprigs being attached to the pulpit. Len Castle of Southtop Farm has a hop-yard, which always strikes me as strange for a 'temperance' man. However, the word is 'temperance'. In a county that produces so much beer 'tee-total' is hardly an acceptable word.

There is only one service at Park Chapel on Sundays, a mid-afternoon service at three o'clock, which is agreed to be the time least likely to disturb the farming routine.

On the afternoon of the Harvest Festival Sunday I left Norton Woodley with my Bible, sermon notes and preaching gown safely stowed in the saddle bag of my bicycle. It was a glorious day. As I crossed the stone bridge over the Leaze, the sparkle of the water was almost too bright to look at. About half a mile out of Norton I took the lane which winds through Dusty Baker's farm. The hedgerows and banks were luscious green and the air was heavy with the scent of wild flowers. I do not know much about wild flowers, but I could recognize the masses of flowering white dead-nettle, the purple thistles and spindly vetch.

Meadows were in clover and some almost yellow with ragwort. Occasionally I glided through shady avenues of trees, dappled with sunlight, and the clicking of my free-wheeling bicycle competed with the sounds of insects, grass-hoppers, crickets, dragon flies, bees, and all the hum and buzz of late summer. There were signs of autumn. Some chestnuts had fallen, their green, prickly spheres lying at the feet of the parent trees, and spattered around the oaks were the first pale, immature acorns. I remember taking deep breaths, drinking it in like nectar, and laughing out loud, feeling so ridiculously happy that I shouted for sheer joy.

I remember asking myself if it were possible for heaven to improve on a country lane in the Woodley Vale, in late summer.

Arriving at the chapel, I found a group of people standing at the door; Len Castle and his wife Mary, Mr and Mrs Eddy Tatton from Hollow Oak Farm, Monica Baker and Clare Trevenna with 'Pip' and 'Squeak', the youngest of the five Trevenna girls. They were all smiling, rather expectantly, like children with a secret. I greeted them, asking Len Castle about his mother, who is housebound. I remembered that after his wife, Marjorie, Eddy Tatton's great love was his prize sow, Sylvie, a large white, whose last litter had presented Eddy with eighteen piglets and the problems of how to feed them and keep them alive. I asked after Sylvie, and only a sharp nudge from Marjorie prevented Eddy from giving me a detailed report.

When I lifted the latch and pushed open the chapel door I was stopped in my tracks. I think I must have gasped. At any rate, there was a buzz of satisfaction from the group at my heels. The chapel was quite literally breathtaking.

The communion table and the communion rails overflowed with every kind of fruit, vegetable and flower; every window-sill, every niche and pew-end was alive with vegetation. The pulpit had disappeared behind a wall of flowers. Only the pulpit lectern top was visible. Each pulpit step had its own harvest decoration. The harmonium, which is on the opposite side to the pulpit, was dripping with greenery and flowers. Mrs Brooks, the organist, sitting at the harmonium, was almost invisible in a floral dress and flower-decked hat. Along the communion rail kneelers were pyramids of apples, plums and pears. Baskets of blackberries were slotted in between sheaves of corn. Wild flowers and hop sprigs were tacked and tied on every beam of wood and every pew-end. Along either side of the central aisle, in trays, trugs, baskets and bowls, was more fruit mixed together with cabbages, carrots, celery, broccoli and runner beans. Wherever I looked there were parsnips, onions, potatoes, cucumbers and marrows.

I suspect that my mouth was open when Eddy Tatton nudged me and said, 'Well, what do 'ee think to that then, minister?' I turned to the smiling group and said, 'I can't say anything, I'm speechless!' 'Ah, well,' said Eddy, giving me a huge wink, 'That's something – 'tis not often we can silence a preacher!'

During the next ten minutes those spaces that were not filled with vegetation gradually became occupied with the sunburned faces of the farming families, together with people from Norton Woodley and a few from Grayleton. Plush cushions had been provided for the Greys and Lord Woodley on the front pew.

Although I have only been in the Woodley Vale circuit a short time, I was surprised at how many faces I could recognize. The hop-growing temperance man, Len Castle, and his wife Joanna were admiring their contribution to the decorations. I could see Monica Baker's cheery face contrasting with the severity of the gaunt John Fielding and his nervous wife, Hetty. Henry and Clare Trevenna were divided by Pip and Squeak. Mrs McBride, looking the country woman she is, sat beside Rene Fletcher, the Norton Woodley Sunday school teacher, whose neat figure betrayed her years in a solicitor's office. Eddy and Marjorie Tatton both looked as pink-faced as their prize pigs; Eddy even has the small, intelligent eyes of the animals of which he is so fond.

There were faces I didn't know. I'd never met Lord Woodley before, although I had met Richard Grey whilst visiting Park Farm, as Dusty is one of Grey's tenants. Monica Baker had also pointed out Nicholas Paine and his wife, in the pew behind the Greys. Paine is the agent and farm manager for the Greys and lives at Grange Gate, the agent's house at Woodley Grange Farm.

One face outstanding for its absence was Dusty Baker's. I could see that there was a space beside Monica, but there was no sign of Dusty.

I announced the first hymn, 'Children of Jerusalem', during the singing of which there was to be a 'procession of produce'. The children of the Park chapel Sunday school were preparing to bring in yet more harvest offerings. Exactly where they were going to put them, I had no idea.

Mrs Brooks began pedalling furiously at the harmonium and eventually the ancient instrument wheezed into asthmatic life and the singing burst forth. The children began to file in. Some carried posies; others, fruit that did not come from local fields, like oranges and bananas, whilst some carried individual items such as a single outsized and knobbly potato, or a massive double-headed tomato.

When we reached the chorus, the whereabouts of Dusty Baker became very clear. He appeared at the door pushing a great wooden wheelbarrow laden with a variety of crops crowned by the largest marrow I have ever seen. He was singing with a voice so loud and harsh that, despite the robust singing of the congregation, it completely overpowered every other voice in the chapel. With a beaming smile his lusty voice gave special value to the chorus of 'Children of Jerusalem'. He attacked the first words like a man sounding the alarm for a fire!

''AARK! 'AARK! 'AARK! whoile infant voices sing. Each ''AARK' produced broad smiles on the faces of the entire congregation. By the time we reached the first 'LOUD!' of 'LOUD 'osannas, LOUD 'osannas', Mrs Brooks had pulled out all the stops and was pedalling for all she was worth, but the harmonium was no match for Dusty. If votes for volume had been taken there would have been a unanimous decision in favour of Dusty's corncrake bellow. By the end of the final chorus, nooks and crannies had been found for all the extra harvest gifts, Dusty's wheelbarrow and marrow taking pride of place across the centre of the aisle near the communion rail.

During this hymn I had carefully negotiated my way into the pulpit, from where I was to lead the congregation in prayer. When Dusty and the children had settled into their seats, I began, 'Let us pray'. At this point the first of the disasters struck. I had laid out my Bible, order of service and sermon notes on top of the pulpit lectern. Having called the congregation to prayer I leaned on the lectern and at that moment discovered that the 'desk' part swivelled. The whole contraption tipped forward and down. I made a grab for my Bible but it was too late. Bible, order of service and sermon notes shot over the lectern top, the notes fluttering down gently, the Bible dropping like a stone and taking with it two vases of flowers which crashed at the feet of Lord Woodley; a third vase merely capsized and in the stunned silence we listened to the water trickling to the floor. Lord Woodley grunted, a kind of 'Humph', but he did not look up. All five Trevenna girls giggled and were promptly 'shushed'. I decided that the best thing to do was to continue. 'Let us pray', I said again.

When I had finished praying I announced the next hymn:

> Come ye thankful people, come,
> Raise the song of harvest home;
> All is safely gathered in
> Ere the winter storms begin.

I did not realize that the vase incident was to be the signal for the beginning of a different kind of storm. The contest between Dusty and the harmonium continued through all four verses of the hymn and then it was Dusty's duty to read the first lesson. He strode up to the reading desk near the harmonium and smiled innocently as the glowing Mrs Brooks arranged her music for the next bout.

He announced the lesson and began to read. He read with as great a vigour as he sang, placing great emphasis on words which he considered significant. It was a dramatic reading, marred only by the fact that he could not cope with a change of column in the printing, or sometimes even a change of line, with the result that he would, by his tone of voice, conclude a statement, only to discover that he was still in the middle of a sentence, the rest of which continued either on the next line, or at the top of the next column. He was also inclined to beat rhythmically, as he read, on the edge of the reading lectern. It was as he was reading the verse, 'And God said, "Behold I . . . have given you every herb yielding . . . seed . . . which is on the face . . . of the earth"' that his time-

34

tapping hand missed the edge of the lectern and crashed into a basket of ripe blackberries. There were more stifled snorts and giggles as Dusty looked at the blackberry juice smeared across his horny hand. He grinned and then continued to read, holding his hand out as if balancing a tray on it. When he had finished the reading he announced the next hymn: 'Yes, God is good, in earth and sky.' Having completed his duty he immediately began to lick his hand, and looked up mischievously when, from her pew, a blushing Monica Baker hissed, 'Dusty!'

The singing of 'Yes, God is good' passed without mishap and when the sensible Marjorie Tatton exchanged places with Dusty at the reading desk, I began to hope that no further incidents were likely. My hopes were to be, almost literally, dashed. The reading was from Matthew 13:

And he spoke to them many thing in parables, saying, 'Behold, the sower went forth to sow.'

Marjorie read clearly and with understanding. She reached the last verse:

He that hath ears, let him hear. 'Oh, my God! Sylvie!'

The last words, which did not sound the least bit Matthean, made me and the entire congregation look up sharply. Marjorie was looking towards the centre aisle which was occupied by the enormous prize-winning sow, mother of eighteen. Eddy Tatton was struggling to get out of his pew. Up to this moment 'Sylvie' had been quietly munching a pew-side cabbage, but Marjorie's accusing voice and the scrabbling of Eddy's Sunday boots had galvanized other pew-holders into action. Several people lunged for the pig, who was startled into a gallop up the aisle scattering the pew-end harvest produce trays, trugs and baskets as she went. Dusty Baker stepped out of his pew at the front and faced the running sow like a matador, or rather, like a traffic policeman, holding up his blackberry-stained hand in the halting position. Sylvie by this time was squealing, obviously terrified by the equally piercing shrieks of the congregation and the yelps of people wno were stumbling over potatoes and falling to the ground behind her. Totally unimpressed by Dusty's hand signal, and seeing no other escape except through his legs, Sylvie did not even hesitate. She ran straight between Dusty's boots and bowled him right over the top of his wheelbarrow. Some people, including myself, think that it was his giant marrow that saved Dusty from serious injury. In any event, his closely-cropped and bullet-shaped head was saved from hitting the floor by the rolling marrow, which neatly cushioned his head at precisely the right moment. From the pulpit I saw it split open on either side of him.

The pig had by now careered into the communion rail, and the pyramids of fruit and vegetables disintegrated and rolled under the feet of the people in the front pews. I looked down at the Grey family and Lord Woodley: the old man was shaking with laugh-

ter, tears streaming down his face. Constance Grey's face was a mixture of concern and suppressed mirth. Richard Grey had thrown his head back, laughing with a curious honking sound.

The commotion ended as suddenly as it had begun, for there was Sylvie quietly gnawing another cabbage. Eddy Tatton picked up the cabbage and coaxed Sylvie out of the church, clearly more concerned for the pig than the prostrate Dusty or the scattered produce. Whilst Eddy was comforting his sow, others were helping Dusty to his feet and gathering up the scattered produce and putting it back into some kind of order. Surprisingly, very little damage was done to the fruit and vegetables. And later, the Norton Woodley Cottage Hospital and the Old People's Home reported it was the finest harvest produce they had ever received.

When it came to the sermon, the notes of which I had lost, long ago it seemed, I decided not to preach at all. I said that there was no need for me to preach, that this congregation and this chapel was its own sermon. We could see how richly we had been blessed both in the harvest of the fields and in the people of the community we lived in, without my philosophizing about it.

I then announced the last hymn, which got quite a laugh. It was, 'We plough the fields and scatter.' As we sang it, Dusty, apparently none the worse for his collision with pig and marrow, had his final joke. His raucous voice could be heard singing, very clearly:

> We plough the fields and *scatter*
> The PRODUCE UP THE AISLE!

The only sad note came when the service was ended. John Fielding marched up to me at the door. He was quite angry. He positively hissed, 'That service was a mockery, a blasphemous mockery! This is supposed to be the house of God!' With that, he took hold of his wife's elbow and hustled her out of the chapel. He clearly did not intend to stay for the harvest tea. I'm afraid John Fielding worries me very much. I really don't know what to do about him. Happily, the Greys and Lord Woodley and everybody else stayed for the tea. To my surprise, Lord Woodley called for me and said, 'My boy, I think I can safely say that that was the most enjoyable Harvest Festival I have ever attended.'

Well, Mr Spoonbill, you did say that if I felt expansive to write freely and any length. I hope you don't mind. I feel that there must be a moral to this story somewhere, but for the life of me, I can't put my finger on it.

With every good wish,

Yours ever,

T. Sefton-Waters

The Manse,
Nether Hadley

My dear Thomas,

How I wish I had been a fly on the wall of the Woodley Park chapel at their Harvest Festival. Your description made it sound hilarious! I have suffered from a variety of similar mishaps in the past, incidents separated over the years, but you seem to have experienced everything that could go wrong, all in the same service!

Enjoy this sense of fellowship and community as long as you can. I have a feeling that it is a way of life that is gradually changing in the name of progress. Many people seem to be moving away from the land, and some of the most beautiful areas of the coast and country are being sold by farmers growing weary of the struggle to make ends meet. Their children are moving away. Sadly, it is not always new farmers who move in but so called developers.

These festivals serve to highlight the mutual concern and fellowship of the community. Your farming families have known each other for generations. When called upon, they will rally round for a neighbour in need. It may not always be so. I fear that what has happened in the towns and cities may well be reflected in the rural areas. People may not merely cease to come to a neighbour's aid, but not even know, or care, who their neighbours are.

The Christian Church has always been a community, the communion of saints, the body of Christ, the fellowship of the kingdom. By which I do not mean a society for the pious and holy. It is the communion of men and women whose only common bond is Jesus Christ. The Church, as the family of Christ, is like any other family, with good and bad children, the devout and those struggling to hold on to their faith by their finger-tips. In fact I would say that the Church is not so much an hotel for the holy, as a hospital for the sick. As a family home, the Church must keep an ever-open door for prodigal children. It is part of our work to keep alive the spirit of community, to help neighbours to care for each other, to bring together brothers and sisters separated by the vagaries of the times we live in. Your community seems, on the surface at least, to be in good spirit. You must work hard to keep that spirit alive.

You have a problem with Mr Fielding. I don't know what it is. You will only find out by attempting to get to know him better. It could be one of many things, or even a combination of several. They do not seem to be a happy couple, he and his wife; that could be at the root of it. He may simply come from a strict and puritanical tradition. It could be his health. He may be in difficulty with his farm, perhaps financially. He may be struggling with his faith. It could be anything. You will have to try to help him. He does not sound the kind of man who would easily accept help, so you will have to be patient and try to win his confidence. It is too easy to dismiss such a person as merely 'an old moaner' who has to be lived with. He and his wife are in as much need of pastoral care as the brightest of the Trevenna children. Whatever it is, his faith does not seem to bring him much comfort or joy, other than the grim satisfaction of confirming his belief that life is a vale of tears.

Well, old warrior, it never ends, does it? There is never a time when a minister can rest on his laurels. Yet there are so many compensations, like your harvest festival.

Thinking again about John Fielding – you need not apologize to him. If he has any Christian charity in him, he should be apologizing to you. Don't expect it. You are likely to be disappointed. It is also likely to take a great deal of time before you can even begin to help him. Whatever you do, do not let his anxieties infect you. When you go through your prayer list tonight, pray for him and put your trust in the

Almighty. Don't lose a moment's sleep over Fielding. When you close your eyes, remind yourself that you are not God. You do not have the answer to everything, nor can you do everything. It is Christ who bears the sins of the world – not you. You are not able. God will give you the strength to cope with your difficulties, at the appropriate time. Never fret in advance.

God bless you Thomas.

Yours ever,

Spoonbill

**The Manse,
Norton Woodley**

Dear Mr Spoonbill,

I called on Mrs Driver yesterday. Her daughter, Frances, who lives in Oakham, is helping to run the shop. She had been helping out during Mr Driver's illness, but now she is having to cope almost single-handedly as Mrs Driver seems to have withdrawn into her grief. She appears unable to concentrate on anything, and she weeps a great deal. Frances wants to hire an assistant, but Mrs Driver says that they cannot afford it. I don't think that is the real reason. I think that she simply doesn't want a 'stranger' working in the bakery. Frances' husband, William, comes over in the evenings to help with the baking, but he is finding it very tiring. He is a gardener at Thirlbury Teacher Training College during the day, and although he is a generous and willing man, the strain is beginning to show.

Mrs Driver says that she wishes she could 'snap out of it', but she can't help herself. She says that she doesn't sleep well, yet in the mornings she finds it difficult to get up, simply because she does not want to face another day. I think she can't come to terms with the reality of death. She has grown up and lived all her life in a Christian community, but she doesn't really know what she thinks about death, resurrection, heaven or hell. She is in a state of bewildered shock.

In our conversations I do my best to bring some light to the questions of what Christians believe about death and resurrection. I can't help thinking that there is a large gap in Mrs Driver's religious education. Somehow she has missed out on these vital questions. I feel that we, the Church, have failed her in her earlier years, through the sin of omission, by simply not facing up to the need to teach about death as part of the process of life. It is not too late for Mrs Driver to come to terms with Christian teaching on this subject, but she is not in the most receptive state of mind just now. However, she is asking questions, even if she appears unable to concentrate on my answers. First of all she wants to know, 'Do I really believe in life after death?' The direct answer to that is, 'Yes, I have staked my life on the resurrection of Christ.' The questions that follow are, 'What does resurrection mean?' and 'Will I actually see Harold again?' To the latter I have given a positive 'Yes', although I had to admit that I do not know 'how' or in exactly what form. We had a look at 1 Corinthians 15 together, which seemed to afford her some relief. I am not sure if Paul's dissertation on the different forms of the resurrected body meant a great deal to her. I think what she found most helpful was Paul's utter conviction about the resurrected life. She also found the opening verses of John 14 helpful; the unequivocal statement that in the Father's house are many rooms, in which a place was being prepared for us. In particular she repeated Christ's words, 'If it were not so, I would have told you.'

Although I can comfort her to some extent by reminding her of the promises of Christ, I wish I could do more to relieve her sense of loss and loneliness.

I know that this is hardly an essay on grief and bereavement, but I hope it will indicate what I believe and where I stand.

Yours ever,

Thomas Selton-Waters

Dear Thomas,

Thank you for your letter about Mrs Driver. I too think that the Church seems to have become somewhat reticent in its preaching about life after death. The idea seems to have developed that we should concentrate on the 'here and now' aspect of life, and leave the 'hereafter' to the hereafter. As a young man, I remember hearing sermons that made the prospect of life after death seem full of excitement. We believed that nothing suffered in this life could diminish the joyful expectations of heaven. I remember sermons in which the preacher evoked images of conversations with ancient heroes and childhood friends and neighbours; and vivid images of the Communion of Saints as a vast fellowship that spanned the centuries. We are living in an age that demands a scientific – sight, touch and proof – religion. Not content with heavenly imagery, it demands earthly evidence, for it is worldly wisdom that must be satisfied.

In one sense there is nothing new in this. In the first chapter of 1 Corinthians Paul speaks about the Gospel as folly to the wise. The Jews demand signs, the Greeks wisdom, but we preach Christ crucified, a stumbling block to the Jews and folly to the Greeks. But to those in Christ that stumbling block and that folly is the power and the wisdom of God – 'Because the foolishness of God is wiser than men; and the weakness of God is stronger than men.'

The entire New Testament doctrine of eternal life is alien to the scientific approach to understanding. I fear that scientists have so astounded us in this century that some churchmen lean over too far backwards to accommodate the scientific approach. I am not saying that scientists are wrong, but I am saying that a first class mathematical brain does not necessarily have a right to make theological pronouncements on the basis of mathematical research. I am also saying that if you laid every scientific discovery, from the beginning of time, at the feet of the creator, they would look insignificant when compared with creation itself. The arrogance of man is not without its humour, to me. It is as if a pipe-smoking, bespectacled frog, having examined a lock of hair, some nail clippings and a finger-print, were to give a dissertation on the mind of the naturalist, or biologist.

If we are unable to preach Christ crucified and risen from the dead, if the resurrection is not true, then we are wasting our time; as Paul says, we might as well 'Eat, drink and be merry, for tomorrow we die.' To live in Christ is to enter the eternal life here and now. Death is a phase through which we pass in the process of eternal life. The sooner we can convince our people that they have already entered the eternal life, the sooner will death and bereavement become surmountable obstacles rather than stumbling blocks. I do not mean that the Christian does not suffer or grieve. Jesus Christ himself wept for Lazarus. Bereavement is traumatically painful. But through the love of Christ we know that mourning will cease and 'every tear shall be wiped away'.

> Love in Christ puts death to flight,
> love prepares the place
> where love, with love will all unite
> before that loving face.

I would like to consider some of the practicalities of ministry to the bereaved. There are all kinds of signs and symptoms to be looked for in those suffering grief. As pastors we minister to the whole person – not only his spiritual difficulties, but also his physical and material problems.

Death is always a shock for the family, whether or not the death was sudden or long expected – the actual moment of separation is deeply disturbing.

We must not be deceived by outward appearances. People frequently present a façade which may well be the exact opposite of their true feelings. Calm cheerfulness may hide deep depression. Sullen and demanding behaviour may mask a desperate need for affection.

Many people develop an unjustifiable sense of guilt, spending an excessive amount of time brooding on 'If only I had done this, or that'.

Loneliness is a major contribution to depression in the bereaved. The older person frequently has few, if any, contemporaries left and is dependent on the younger generation for visits – and luckily, in a community such as yours, young relatives are near. It can be different in the cities.

In middle age loneliness can also be acute. People are embarrassed by death and bereavement. They do not know what to do, or what to say to a friend in grief; they are not being deliberately unkind, but out of embarrassment they avoid what might be an uncomfortable meeting. So that a youngish woman who was once socially active within a group of couples is suddenly cut off by the death of her husband. She is not visited by her old friends. She is not invited to people's homes and she herself feels incapable of rebuilding a social life.

The single person who has spent many years looking after an elderly relative is often numbed by the emptiness of her days, although in time there is frequently a sense of release, and a completely new life becomes possible.

Children can be deeply disturbed, if only because adults are afraid to tell them the truth. Those who send their children away until the funeral is over frequently deprive their children of a valuable, emotionally maturing experience. Children need to share in the family's emotional upheaval. If children are not sent away they are often silenced or discounted on the grounds that they are 'too young to understand', when in fact their spontaneous reactions and assessments are often able to clarify the confused mind of the adult. The reality of death should not be hidden from children; such a deprivation is more likely to harm than protect. By sharing in the family experience they are drawn closer to other members of the family. They are better able to accept the reality of death surrounded by the love of the family. Children are far more resilient than we allow, and do have the capacity to understand and accept the naturalness of death. However, they must be supported by the love and assurance of the family, for otherwise the death of a close relative can be dangerously disturbing.

As pastors we must be aware of the whole family, not only at the time of the bereavement but also in the long days and weeks in which the bereaved struggle to come to terms with their loss. We must visit the bereaved, talk with them, listen to them and pray with them. We must be prepared to give them time. A 'quick' visit may salve the conscience, but it gives the bereaved no opportunity to unburden themselves.

Lay members of the church have an important ministry to offer the bereaved. A visit from a class leader, or a member of a church fellowship, will be greatly appreciated. Their visit, however, must not be substituted for a visit from the minister. Our people do expect their ministers to be mediators, links, to bring the word of God to their situation. It is a fearsome responsibility which we cannot, ultimately, delegate. Because of this responsibility we are frequently with people in their moment of crisis. Because this is our calling we will continue to share these experiences throughout the years of our ministry. As our experience increases we notice patterns of behaviour. As we become accustomed to grief, we become knowledgeable in a way that cannot be expected of those who do not have the privilege of sharing so frequently in the deepest experiences of so many people.

We need to be genuinely concerned for people if we are to help them practically as well as spiritually. A few well-chosen prayers are not enough; we must minister to the whole person. Let me consider some of the most common 'symptoms' of distress in bereavement. I have mentioned feelings of guilt. The most common guilt is that of neglect, and almost as frequent is deep regret for heated and unkind words in past moments of conflict. There is a tendency to relive these moments, as if the survivor is trying to punish himself for his guilt. Whilst this reaction is not surprising, it can easily become a self-indulgent wallowing.

Hostility towards doctors and nurses is also a common occurrence, with soul-destroying attempts to attribute blame. This kind of hostility is frequently accompanied by phrases such as, 'He would have been alive today if . . .' Sometimes the bereaved is filled with a desire to take legal action. This is almost invariably an unwise, unhealthy and unhelpful exercise which can only hurt. For anyone to enter into litigation whilst emotionally disturbed by grief is something that is best avoided. Hostility coupled with guilt can be extremely dangerous, for then the hostility can turn inwards and lead to despair and even suicide.

Sometimes there is an obsession with the memory of the person who has died which amounts almost to an inability to accept what has happened. It can be seen in various ways, such as 'keeping his room exactly as it was when he was alive', 'setting his place at table'. (Though this often happens accidentally, from habit.) 'Seeing' her face in a crowd, 'hearing' his voice in company: these are common signs of inability to come to terms with the fact of death.

Most common, and usually to be expected, is the feeling of 'distance' from other people; restlessness, aimlessness, inability to complete simple tasks or even sentences.

What then can we do? We can visit, and in our visits listen and talk with patience. We can encourage people to come to terms with their experience and to make a life for themselves, even when they can see no point in going on. People often say, 'I will never be the same again; I feel as though half of me has died.' In a sense they are right; they will never be the same again. There is no absolute cure for grief. They have been deeply wounded in the battle. However, wounds can heal; they may leave a scar, but in time we can learn to live with them. During this healing period, the minister and the church members must do all they can to ease the bereaved person's loneliness.

People vary in their ability to cope with bereavement. One can hardly work out a timetable for grief but, if it does not seem too clinical to say so, I think that usually, in the case of someone losing their life-time partner it takes about two years for people to *begin* to be able to live with their loss, or as people often say '. . . to feel *normal* again'. As I have said, loving support during this time is essential.

If there is no attempt to overcome the depression of

grief, then deep morbidity will develop. In elderly people in particular it can mean the loss of the will to live and, as people used to say, they can 'die of a broken heart'.

Your Mrs Driver is struggling back on the road to life. She is weeping, and emotional release is a necessary part of recovery. She is asking questions, she is finding the faith she has always had, and with your help will grow stronger. In time you may be able to challenge her to renew and recommit herself to the love of God. Eventually you might be able to help her to find fulfilment either within the Church or the community. Eventually she may be able to use her experience to help others.

In Christ we are all on the road to 'our Father's' house, and the trials of today are eased in the knowledge that we are surrounded by people who care for us and love us, and in the knowledge that God is a loving Father who suffers with us, dies with us, and prepares a place for us and all those who love and trust him.

I'm sorry that I have rambled on, and not presented my thoughts in a neat, textbook-like manner, but there we are. We all have our limitations.

Yours ever,

W. Spoonbill

Dear Mr Spoonbill,

I feel I must talk to you about a young people's group in the church – it's worrying me, or rather my own feelings about it are worrying me. The Young People's Fellowship conducted our evening service last Sunday. Two youngsters, a boy and a girl, 'gave their witness'. I've always found this kind of public declaration of an individual's spiritual progress hard to take; it's quite embarrassing, in fact. I'm sure the fault lies in me, but try as I might I can't rid myself of the distaste I feel. I hope this doesn't mean that I'm some sort of spiritual prig, but it's very difficult for me to control my feelings of scepticism. For instance, from their accounts they were apparently, before 'conversion', incredibly wicked, but now they are paragons of virtue who seem to walk about two inches above the earth, with permanent smiles. Looking at their bright-eyed and fresh faces I simply do not believe that they know anything about real wickedness.

They have also 'solved' everything. They have no doubts about anything, no fears, no questions. The Incarnation, the Resurrection, Heaven, Hell – the Bible answers everything. I wish it did for me.

We had tea in the Fellowship leader's cottage. The leader, Herbert Mitchell, read an article: 'Science proves the Bible'.

I'm afraid I left as soon as it was decently possible.

I am sorry that this letter is so short, but it's rather late and I must turn in.

Best wishes,

Yours,

T. Sefton-Waters

The Manse,
Nether Hadley

Dear Thomas,

Tread carefully with your Young People's Fellowship! 'Giving a witness' has very good biblical precedent: the great St Paul 'gave witness' many times. It is a perfectly valid way of declaring one's faith. It is true, however, that in the telling and retelling of one's personal story there is a temptation to expand and embroider. Past sins are, perhaps unconsciously, painted blacker for the sake of contrast with the new state.

As for fresh-faced innocents knowing little about real evil, you should be grateful for that. Whilst you may be aware of all kinds of wickedness and depravity, and the longer you are a minister the more you will learn, you must allow that sin and wickedness take their proportions from the mind and experience of the sinner. What may seem to you to be a minor sin against truthfulness may seem to the sinner to be an act of gross treachery. Never undervalue another's experience simply because it is not as lusty as your own. If these boys and girls were your own children you would not dismiss their confessions by saying, 'Ho, Ho – wait until you have really sinned – as I have!'

As to taking a stand against a fundamentalistic approach to the Bible, I cannot but agree that you should make your position clear. To smile benignly, or to sit in suffering silence, whilst people pour out all kinds of theological rubbish is a deceitful form of spiritual cowardice. I suspect that we clergy have a lot to answer for with regard to the damage we have done by not being theologically honest, by concealing what we really believe. I have heard it said that, theologically, the pew is usually fifty yards behind the pulpit. If that is true then it is our duty to reduce the gap.

I think you should not have left the young people drinking in the 'science proves the Bible' talk without a comment from you. You need not be aggressive. A few probing questions would be as effective as an outright attack. A statement to the effect that whilst you find these 'scientific' observations interesting, your faith does not depend on scientific discovery but on spiritual experience and exploration centred on the person of Christ. Such a statement might, at the very least, have the effect of putting the 'scientific' talk into perspective; at the best it could help the young people to see what is really central to Christian faith.

You will have to come to terms with your Fellowship leader sooner or later, so why not sooner? It is as important to attempt to open *his* mind as it is to enlighten the young people, perhaps more so. The real question is, if you intend to knock away the legs of the fundamentalist argument, what are you going to put in its place? May I suggest an approach? I believe a positive challenge that will stimulate *thought* is always preferable to negative criticism. Challenge your young people to dig deeper! Challenge them to become detectives, theological sleuths! Tell them what you know to be true, that life is a continuous exploration, an ongoing search; that the religious life is a series of discoveries, that even when they are pensioners they will still be on the nursery slopes of discovery; that the excitement of being alive is not arriving at destinations but making the journey; that to stop searching is to have stopped living. In a word, do not dismay them with doubt but excite them with curiosity.

Battle on, old warrior!

Spoonbill

Dear Mr Spoonbill,

Herbert Mitchell, the Young People's Fellowship leader, called at the manse at lunch time.

He seems to sense that I am not very supportive about his Fellowship activities. He said that he had hoped that Sunday night would have been a good opportunity to have 'sealed them in the faith of the Lord'. He felt that his 'science proves' talk had laid the foundations for me to have confirmed the truth that the Bible is the inspired word of God.

He was deeply disappointed that I had left so early.

I tried to explain that as my opinions about 'science proves' were not the same as his I did not want to have an argument with him in front of the young people. I noticed that the news that I had different opinions from his caused him some barely controlled consternation. He was clearly perplexed and I think that he has gone away suspecting that I am not what he would call a 'real Christian'. I'm afraid that he is not very happy with the new minister.

I don't know, I hardly seem to have put my foot in the door and I'm already crossing swords.

Yours ever,

T. Sefton-Waters

My dear Thomas,

You may have crossed swords, but I think your Fellowship leader is winning on points. You must stop parrying and fight back! Stand your ground! Hoist your colours! Take up the gauntlet!

Let us start with that vexed expression, 'The inspired word of God'. What does it mean? It seems to me that some people's concept of the Bible as 'the inspired word of God' embraces the rather fanciful notion that God dictated the Bible, word for word. This idea is reduced to absurdity if we ask the question, 'How did the writers take down the divine dictation?' Did they use the demotic or hieratic form of shorthand, or did they merely ask the Almighty to speak more slowly, or in the case of Moses chiselling on stone, extremely slowly? Actually Moses had an easier time of it than most, he didn't chisel on stone: it was written on its tablets for him by the finger of God! The interesting question is, 'What language did the Almighty use?' Until about 750 B.C. the Israelites had no written language. When they did invent a written language, it had no vowels. How then was the Bible written?

As you undoubtedly know, Thomas, the tribes depended on the oral tradition. One must not underrate the accuracy of the oral tradition. For people who have no written language, accuracy in retelling the stories of their culture is extremely important. It is only in a modern 'literate' society where there is no tradition of an accurate oral history, where because of books we have less need to cultivate the art of memorizing, that the Colonel's message, 'Send reinforcements, we are about to advance', whispered from soldier to soldier, reaches headquarters as, 'Send three and fourpence, we're going to a dance.' How then was the Bible written? Clearly, it is a compilation of both written and oral traditions. The writers consist of a great variety of ordinary and not so ordinary human beings, from poets to soldiers, from housewives to kings, who struggled to find the words that would express the truth that had been revealed to them by God through physical and spiritual experience.

The details of a biblical passage, the styles of writing, the devices employed, though fascinating, are none the less secondary to the meaning of the passage and the intention of the writer. You must convince your young people that it is more important to understand the text thoroughly than it is to be able to quote the words of a particular translation. It is the truth contained in the biblical stories that is 'inspired' – not the literal words.

For example, in the non-biblical story of the boy who cried, 'Wolf!' when there was no wolf; who roused people with false alarms so often that when he cried, 'Wolf' in earnest, no one responded to his cries because they no longer believed him, the meaning of the story, or the truth contained, is that, ultimately 'lies' rebound upon the liar. If I were to change the details, if I said it was not a boy, but a girl, it was not a wolf but a lion and the story happened on a Tuesday rather than a Wednesday, these details would not alter the 'truth' contained in the story: that lying will get you into trouble.

The Book of Genesis begins with the words, 'In the beginning God created the heavens and the earth.' There, in a single sentence, is the 'truth' about the creation story. It is followed by a very sophisticated *attempt*, by primitive people, to explain 'how' God made heaven and earth – a question still being debated by scientists. Whether or not the biblical writers were scientifically accurate in their attempts to define 'how' God created the world, is of secondary importance. The *inspired* truth lies in the first sentence, 'In the beginning, God created . . .' Let us leave 'how' he did it to the scientists.

The Bible is not a scientific text book, or a geography primer, or even a history book. The writers are frequently inaccurate and often contradictory in these matters. The Bible is not an infallible book to be slavishly followed word for word. It is a massive collection of prose narrative, poetry, songs, adventure stories, flights of imagination and even fantasy. The inspired truths are expressed in many forms, and because the writers were human beings they wrote with varying degrees of success. To commit yourself to a fundamentalist's approach to the Bible is to suspend your God-given powers of reason and intelligence.

In Methodism we believe that the Bible contains all that is necessary for salvation. That does not mean that the Bible cannot be questioned, or retranslated or reinterpreted.

If your Fellowship leader suggests, as I suspect he might, that you are destroying the simple faith of the young people, then because I think that faith so easily destroyed is hardly worth having, I would have to say that I would rather have an honest doubter than a believer with a closed mind. It is your duty to encourage enquiring minds, to build faith that actively seeks and enquires, an intelligent faith that does not exist merely for comfort and consolation, but grows through experience and knowledge. As St Anselm puts it in only three words (an example to us all), *Fides Quaerens Intellectum.*

My reference to St Anselm is not a subtle reminder that I have not yet received your essay on the medieval schoolmen.

Yours ever,

Spoonbill

The Second Year

The Manse,
Norton Woodley

Dear Mr Spoonbill,

I had to visit a very sick woman in hospital today. She is paralysed from the neck down. She has been in hospital for a very long time, over a year. I must confess that I was very worried about meeting her. She's going through a terrible ordeal. She lies in a plaster cast, on her back for four hours, then a plaster cast is placed over her, secured with leather straps and she's turned over and spends the next four hours on her front. This goes on continually, day and night, week after week and month after month.

The more I thought about it the more concerned I became about what comfort I could possibly offer her. What could I say to her? Even common small talk became more and more meaningless when I considered it. I wondered if I would even be able to say, 'How are you?' Expressions like 'How do you feel?' would hardly be appropriate in these particular circumstances. How cosy those Pastoral Theology discussions on 'visiting the sick' seem when I look back on them. In plain words, I felt even more inadequate than I usually do.

What happened was an experience that lifts my spirits even as I attempt to write these notes, and I suspect that my spirit will be lifted whenever I think about this meeting for the rest of my life. I did not comfort Mrs Parker, she comforted me. Mrs Parker ('Call me Ethel, dear, everyone does . . .'), took the initiative from the moment we met. She asked me about myself, my family, my college, the manse, she appeared to have an insatiable curiosity and a genuine interest in the new minister. She is so alive. She has a sparkle in her eye because of her wonderful sense of humour. She reads a great deal, when she is on her back. They have provided her with a frame on which a book can be placed and because she can move her head she is able to turn the pages with a stick held between her teeth. When she was explaining this she made a joke about liking to 'get her teeth into a good book'. Last Christmas she sent a greetings card to every Methodist minister overseas. As a result she received cards from all over the world. She winked at me and said, 'I collect foreign stamps, so you see, I'm not so daft as I'm funny looking!' Her courage is breathtaking. She told me about her prayers. She said, 'I don't ask to be cured any more, I just ask for strength to get through the day.' She seems to know everyone in the hospital. No one passes by without Ethel calling out to them. Just before I left she said I would have to become a missionary and then I could send her a regular supply of foreign stamps. It almost seems a good enough reason for going overseas.

When I left I felt buoyant, lifted up. She had comforted me rather than the other way about. Leaving her was like stepping out of a magic circle. It is as if she is surrounded by an aura of happy vitality. I simply can't explain it. It was an extraordinary experience.

I'm not sure that, having visited her, I am any the wiser about the problem of suffering. I had the feeling that I was late in stepping into her arena. She seems to have won the battle already. I don't really know what to think. It seems incredible, but she has left me bewildered and elated at one and the same time.

Yours ever,

T. Sefton-Waters

The Manse,
Nether Hadley

My dear Thomas,

How absolutely marvellous! You have been extremely fortunate. You really have been blessed. Suffering can embitter and destroy some people, with others, like Mrs Parker, suffering is brought to heel. It may imprison the body but it fails utterly to imprison the spirit. I think you are perfectly correct in your sense of awe in her presence, or at least in the presence of the power within her that is enabling her to cope with her suffering. I doubt if I will ever be able to give you a Christian apology for suffering that will come within a stone's throw of Mrs Parker's testimony. I'm afraid I cannot hope to understand fully the depth of her experience. You will learn far more from listening and talking to this lady than you ever will from me. I wish I had a mustard seed of her faith. It is faith like hers that brings pharisees like us down to earth.

I can appreciate your trepidation at the thought of visiting someone who is suffering greatly. To attempt to bring comfort to the suffering is one of the chief responsibilities of a minister. It is a task that we can never attempt to avoid. As servants of Christ, called to the pastoral ministry, it is our privilege, a formidable privilege, to be with people in all kinds of crises, in times of trial, in sickness of mind and body, in temptation, in coping with success and in the face of death. Paul in his second letter to the Corinthians (2 Corinthians 1:3 & 4) says, 'Blessed be the God and Father of our Lord Jesus Christ, the Father of mercies and God of comfort; who comforteth us in all our affliction, that we may be able to comfort them that are in any affliction, through the comfort wherewith we ourselves are comforted of God.' Sadly the word 'comfort' has become something of a milksop word, it has lost a great deal of its original meaning, that is the literal meaning, com-fort – with strength. The word 'comfort' is really a close relation of the word 'fortify'. To 'comfort' in the true sense does not mean merely to 'sympathize', it means 'to strengthen'.

The difficulty for us is that it is almost impossible to talk about suffering, without at the same time considering providence, sin, creation, the nature of God, or for that matter, the existence of God. All I can possibly do here is to consider some of the questions.

First, let me say that in the face of suffering, that is in the presence of people in actual pain, a monologue on the Christian theology of suffering is not what is required. At that moment people need the encouragement of your faith, the security of your love, the promise of hope in what you do and what you are. In these moments, what you *are* is far more important than anything you might *say*. Having said that, we must accept that what you are depends on what you believe. So let us consider our beliefs in this area.

People often say that they cannot believe in a loving God when there is so much suffering in the world, yet, paradoxically, a world without suffering might well be a world without love. I say 'might' because it may be possible, for some, to know joy without pain, laughter without tears or to appreciate light without much knowledge of the dark. However, consider a world in which man was incapable of being unloving, a world in which we had no choice about loving or not loving. If you could not choose to love, would love, as we understand it, exist? If you could not choose to sin, would your inevitably sinless actions be worthy or good? If there was no such thing as suffering would there be such a thing as compassion? What sort of creature would man be if he were incapable of choosing to love, had no knowledge of doing good and no awareness of the nature of compassion? Undoubtedly, he would be a lesser being than man as we know him now.

Very often moral evil and suffering are treated as one problem. We are inclined to believe that all suffering is evil. I am afraid it cannot be as simple as that. There is a difference between mental and physical suffering. For example, we might suffer from an uneasy conscience, which is not necessarily a bad thing.

There are those who argue that all suffering is not real, it is all in the mind. Mary Baker Eddy taught that 'mind' was the only reality and 'matter' an illusion. Suffering and death, she said, are the effects of false thinking. The Christian Scientists are great advocates of the idea that there is nothing good or bad but thinking makes it so. The trouble is I *do* think, and thoughts are real, including evil thoughts. Why should I have them if they are not real? I also think I feel pain. Do you know the limerick on this subject?

> There was a young lady from Deal
> Who thought that pain wasn't real,
> But when I prick my skin
> With the end of a pin,
> I dislike what I fancy I feel.

It is very complicated and puzzling. We cannot say that good can come out of all suffering even though in Christ we see that the love of God was revealed through the suffering of the Passion. There have been many arguments put forward in an attempt to save God's reputation in the matter of suffering. Unfortunately, like Mary Baker Eddy and the Christian Scientists, they produce rather weak theology if not outright heresy. For instance, there are those who say that good and evil are ultimate things, and because of this the Devil is unavoidable. But this is not acceptable to Christian thought, there is only one ultimate, one creator. We can't have it both ways, one God and two creators!

Some say that God has failed to realize his purpose for man and is now trying, by the improvement and progression of man, to put things right. It's a mildly attractive thought, though it is inclined to reduce the Almighty to a bumbling amateur who might eventually get it right. This argument of course is an attempt to make God in the image of man.

No, I'm afraid that these theories to save God's reputation run the risk of destroying God. The easiest answer is to say that there is no God, to take a fatalistic stance and say, you are either lucky or you are not. The problem of evil only arises then for the believer in God. Well, we who do believe, what shall we do – go on trying to find an excuse for God?

I believe that we must accept that God knew what he was doing when he created the world as it is, allowing and admitting that our not understanding is not the same as not accepting. Even though we may not understand fully yet I think it is possible to 'see through a glass darkly'. What things do we see 'darkly'?

First, I think we can see those areas of suffering where man can be held responsible for a great deal of pain of the world. If by 'evil' we mean 'moral evil' then it is very clear that man has been, and no doubt will continue to be, very responsible. A tremendous amount of suffering is the direct result of moral evil. I do not need to give examples of suffering caused through greed, envy, lust for power or common self-ishness.

Again, much suffering is the result of ignorance. Nature also contributes to the world's sum of misery; children and the innocent fall foul of ignorance and disease. Here we must ask, is ignorance evil? Is our ignorance of how to treat disease culpable ignorance? If man spends his wealth on warfare and prestige at the expense of medical research, is his medical ignorance therefore culpable ignorance, resulting in the unnecessary prolonging of suffering? However, we cannot blame ourselves for earthquakes, storms and floods. Some say that when man fell, nature fell also, but I must confess that I find this meaningless.

One of the most common superstitions is that all suffering is in proportion to man's evil. So often people say, 'What have I done to deserve this?', as if their suffering was a punishment for past sins. People find it hard to accept the world as it is. The Bible says 'it rains on the just and the unjust'. Virtue does not keep you dry, nor does it make you immune from disease, nor did it protect Jesus Christ from the agony of Gethsemane.

What then can we say, as Christians, about suffering? First, we must do all in our power to fight moral evil, in the world and in ourselves. We must be involved in the battle to reduce unnecessary suffering, we must combat the abuse of nature. We must accept the world as it is, in the sense that it is inevitable that certain things will happen to us. We will all grow old. Our bodies will, in some cases, break down, wear out, cease to function. We will all face death. We can, however, face these things with more than mere stoicism.

When you were describing your visit to Mrs Parker, the paralysed lady, you said, 'It is as if she is surrounded by an aura . . .' I think that is possibly an accurate description of what you experienced. I don't know if I can put into words exactly what I mean, but I will try.

Whenever we face great suffering, it is likely that we will pray, like Our Lord in the Garden of Gethsemane, 'Father, if it is possible, take this cup from me.' Now sometimes our problems are not as great as we thought, and perhaps our prayers are answered through the balm of friendship, medicine or of that great healer, time. Sometimes it seems as if our prayers are not answered, and our problem remains, and all we can do is go through it, or live with it. The answer to Christ's prayer was not the removal of his agony, but the revelation that he possessed the power not only to face what lay before him but also the power to triumph over the worst that man can do to man, the power to triumph over sin and death itself. When you stood at the bedside of Mrs Parker, and became aware of her courage, her humour, her spirit, you were indeed standing within a special 'aura'. I think you were standing in the presence of the power that took Christ through the crucifixion. That is why I said that you will learn more from listening to that lady than you ever will from me. Of course, there is no way to 'explain' suffering, or the mind of the creator when this wild, mad, beautiful, and astonishing world came into being, but I do know this, 'it is the best of all possible worlds for making saints'.

'For I am persuaded, that neither death, nor life, nor angels, nor principalities, nor things present, nor things to come, nor powers, nor height, nor depth, nor any other creature, shall be able to separate us from the love of God, which is in Christ Jesus our Lord.'

God bless you, Thomas,

Spoonbill

Dear Mr Spoonbill,

I think I have always spoken warmly of Dusty and Monica Baker. Of all the people in the Woodley Vale they have been the friendliest and the most hospitable. It is always a pleasure to visit them at Park Farm. They are such a lively family. Dusty is so full of humour and goodwill. Although they are in their fifties, he and Monica lark about as if they were in their twenties.

Monica is an immensely practical woman, able to turn her hand to anything the farm demands. The farm poultry is entirely her responsibility and she has the whole operation organized to perfection. She is an excellent cook, a good horsewoman and she is also able to drive a car, lorry or tractor if the need arises.

They have four children, three boys and a girl. The oldest boys are twins, Tom and Tim. Both are obsessed with things mechanical. They are usually to be found in some shed or barn either dismantling a motorcycle or rebuilding a tractor engine, or inventing a machine that will transfer a stock of mangolds from the upper floor of a shed to the back of a trailer. Not surprisingly, they want to set themselves up in business as specialists in agricultural machinery, supplies and repairs. The youngest boy, Will, is twelve years old and, of course, is still at school. When he is not at school he is usually about twelve inches away from his father, wherever he may be, whether Dusty is in a field, on a tractor or herding cattle. The oldest child is their daughter, Sally. She is a student, in her final year, reading English at Bristol University.

It is really Sally that I want to talk about. I hope it won't come as a shock to you, especially as I have been in Woodley Vale only a little more than a year, but, well I can't think of a gentle way of saying it, so I might as well put it bluntly. We are engaged to be married.

We met last Christmas when the Bakers invited me to spend Christmas Day with the family. Christmas at Park Farm was a marvellous experience, quite apart from meeting the girl I intend to marry. It was one of the happiest days I can ever remember. It seemed to overflow with the spirit of Christmas. There was so much laughter, good food, carols and songs at the piano. They made me feel that I was one of the family, and with these people that was a great privilege.

Sally seems to my prejudiced eye to have inherited the best qualities of Dusty and Monica. She has her mother's handsome looks, her gift of practical versatility and her father's infectious sense of humour. There is, however, something about her that is entirely her own. There is a quietness about her, a secret smile that conceals the thoughts behind her behaviour as a dutiful daughter. Her horizons are much wider than the Woodley Vale farming community. She is not wedded to any particular party politics, but she has a sensitive social awareness, a genuine concern for people. She wants to travel and is very interested in my thoughts about working in overseas missions.

I know that all this must sound as if I am running before I can walk, but Sally and I have had long discussions and we have both been thinking and praying about our future together. It does look as if we might make a good team, though that thought was not consciously in my mind when I proposed to her. Exactly what thought processess were at work I have no idea. They are too deep for me to analyse, even if I wanted to. I simply thought, and continue to think, that she is the most wonderful girl I have ever met. During her last weekend at home, nearly a month ago now, I proposed and to my delighted amazement she accepted immediately. Mr and Mrs Baker know of our engagement, and I have written to my parents, but before we made it public knowledge I felt that I must let you know first.

I am aware that I would require special permission to marry before my ordination, and also that it would be wiser for Sally to graduate first. So perhaps we should wait until my ordination in two years' time.

Although we have not 'announced' our engagement, I wonder if the effect of it is noticeable to the people of Woodley Vale. It seems to have filled me with an energy I did not know I possessed. Either my bicycle is running very smoothly or I am getting extremely fit, I seem to be speeding around the villages and farms on my visits as if the bike had been motorized!

Even the Bible seems to have taken on a new significance. The passages of my daily readings suddenly appear to have become more vital, and my sermon preparation does not seem such a chore, in fact I feel as if I have inspiration for a dozen sermons!

Last Sunday Dusty said, 'That was one of the most cheerful sermons I have ever heard, Tom.' Then he gave me what was meant to be a sly wink, but because there is nothing sly about Dusty it became a signal that I felt the entire congregation must have witnessed, especially when he added, 'It must be the weather – or somethin'!' He is right of course, the climate of the heart is at this moment considerably sunnier than the weather we have been enjoying lately.

With every good wish,
Yours ever,

Thomas Sefton-Waters

Dear Thomas,

Congratulations! What wonderfully exciting news. Sally sounds a marvellous girl. Having such a positive effect on your work she must be exceptionally right for you. God bless you both.

I am sure you are right about waiting for Sally to graduate, it would be far too disturbing for both of you to consider anything else. As to waiting for two years, until after your ordination, I am sure about that too. If your offer to serve overseas is accepted, and I can think of no reason why it should not be, then there might be some distinct advantages in marrying immediately after your ordination.

There is a preparation course for ministers intending to serve overseas, and where possible, wives are also encouraged to take part in the course. Apart from learning about the country you will be living in, it means that you would both have a headstart in learning the language required. The course is, I understand, quite comprehensive, for some overseas stations require the minister to be a Jack of all trades. In which case I think that the ministerial training department might consider marriage immediately after ordination positively desirable. If you would like me to sound them out for you, please let me know.

From your point of view, marriage to a girl like Sally can only be beneficial, but I wonder if she knows exactly what she is letting herself in for? I am sure she does, in general if not in particular. She comes from a family that had been devoted to the service of the Church for generations, and who are undoubtedly aware of the demands of the ministry.

She is, as you say, a concerned and committed person, and it sounds as if she would enjoy being of service to both the Church and the community. On the other hand, she has a mind of her own, her own special talents and perhaps a desire to specialize along lines of her own choosing. In some situations she might find church duties somewhat irksome and restrictive.

In my opinion the Church expects rather too much of ministers' wives. They are an unpaid workforce, or as some say, unpaid curates. I can think of very few other callings in which a man's wife is expected to be an unpaid member of staff, a secretary, counsellor and hostess. So many churches consider that it is 'normal' for the minister's wife to be president of the 'Young Wives' Fellowship', to chair the 'Women's Bright Hour' and assist the Girl Guides, or any other women's organization that exists in the local church.

Of course, none of these things are obligatory, but she will find that the pressures exist for her to assume these or similar roles. Many women welcome these tasks and gain a great deal from them, not least a sense of joy and purpose. A minister, and the church, is indeed fortunate if his wife actually wants to do these things, but I really think that we should not expect it as a matter of course.

As for the overseas work, I think that the Mission

House would want you to think very hard if your wife is not prepared to support you in this wholeheartedly. In the mission field you really would have to work as a team.

Another thing you will have to consider, even if it seems rather a long way off at the moment, is the education of your children. Much will depend on which country you are working in; you may find that an excellent educational system is available. The Methodist church does have some very good boarding schools in this country, and financial assistance would be given to a minister serving overseas; in fact every minister, wherever he is serving, is given assistance if he considers a boarding school education the best thing for his children.

However, we have leapt into the future! You are not even married yet! Still, it is important to bear these things in mind when you and Sally are making your plans.

This does give us a splendid opportunity to discuss the institution of marriage, and Christian marriage in particular. I won't launch into that right now, it might take the gilt off the gingerbread! For the moment I just want to send you every blessing and to assure you of my prayers. Once again, congratulations. Wherever else you may go in the world, you are now sure to remember Norton Woodley for the rest of your life.

God bless you both (you see I'm already thinking of you in the plural!)

Yours ever,

Walter Spoonbill

Dear Mr Spoonbill,

Thank you for your encouraging letter about our engagement. I would indeed be very grateful if you would make some enquiries about the possibility of our marrying before ordination in order that we might prepare together for work overseas.

Curiously, as a kind of counter-balance to our happiness, I've recently been talking to a woman whose divorce has just been finalized. When she called I don't think that she knew exactly what she wanted to say, I think that she just wanted someone with whom she could talk things over as dispassionately as possible.

She was obviously distressed. Her marriage had reached the point of no return a long time ago, and she thought that she had come to terms with the hard facts, but now that the final divorce papers have come through, it is as if the wound had been reopened.

She's quite convinced that neither of them would have been happy, even if her husband had come back. She has been through and through the agony of choosing what she believes will be the lesser pain, nevertheless she is suffering a great sense of loss – almost as if she had been bereaved.

She says that she feels discarded, like a worn-out garment that has been cast onto a rubbish heap. It is not only the final break from her husband that depresses her, but the fact that despite her being the 'injured' party, her old friends seem to be avoiding her as if she was, as she says, 'unclean'.

She lives in the market town of Newton St John. She is an Anglican, but since the breakdown of her marriage she has felt unable to worship and suspects that she would not really be welcomed in her local church. She and her husband have no children, which may have something to do with the breakdown of their marriage, I don't know. She didn't discuss the cause of the breakdown, although she frequently referred to herself as, 'the injured party'. I gather that her husband simply moved out of their home and never returned. The grounds for divorce were infidelity. It seems that her husband did not contest the petition, in fact he appears to have provided the evidence against himself. It was impossible to get to the bottom of it all, she was too distressed and confused for me to press her with questions. Mainly I just listened whilst she talked. I have invited her to call again, whenever she wants to – she seemed grateful for that. I didn't feel that I was particularly helpful; there didn't seem much that I could offer her in the way of comfort. I would be glad of your comments.

Yours ever,

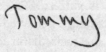

Tommy

Dear Tommy,

Thank you for your letter. I am sure that you were right to do little more than listen to your divorced visitor. It is not wise to come to decisions when you know so little about the people involved. In this instance it seems that the time for reconciliation, if there ever was such a time, is long past. Mrs X is at the bottom of a steep cliff, her descent to this position has been extremely painful, and she may have suffered permanent injury. At the top of the cliff is some semblance of 'normal' life, her problem is that she neither knows the route to the top, nor is she in the best of physical and spiritual condition to even begin the climb. She refers to herself as the 'injured' party, which is no doubt true, but injury and innocence must not be confused. If she is to be restored to health then she will have to come to terms with the fact that in the breakdown of a marriage there is rarely a totally innocent party. I am not being judgemental, but stating what I believe to be a fact about human relationships.

In some ways the complete breakdown of a marriage is very similar to bereavement. In other ways it can be even worse than bereavement. The bereaved can look back on happy days and be afforded the comfort of the memory of a lasting relationship. For the divorced it is difficult for such memories not to be tinged with bitterness.

The bereaved may regret many things and may frequently think, 'if only I had done this or that', but the finality of death ultimately reduces this regret because we know that the person for whom we grieve cannot come back. In a marriage breakdown the hope might never be totally extinguished, however improbable the possibility of reconciliation.

For some, divorce can be more damaging than bereavement because it is coupled with a sense of frustration and failure. It is not only the loss of someone you have loved but the loss of the love that once motivated your life. In bereavement, love has not died.

Her feelings of being discarded and thrown onto a rubbish heap are similar to those of being physically beaten and robbed, because it is as if all the dreams that she had cherished had been snatched from her; as if all the years that had been put into the building of her marriage were like the twigs of a child's make-believe house, kicked apart and scattered by bullies. Of course, if she is able to come to a true assessment of those years, they are far from wasted, the difficulty lies in (forgive the pun) 'picking up the pieces' and making something out of what is left, and then finding the will to build a new 'house'.

I am sorry that so many of her friends have deserted her in her hour of need. It is, not unnaturally, difficult for those who were mutual friends of both Mr and Mrs X. One can understand their embarrassment, but it all goes towards increasing her feelings of hurt and loneliness. When she feels strong enough, she may have to make the first approaches to her old friends and run the risk of discovering which are the real friends and which are not.

I am especially sorry that she finds it impossible to go to her local church, but it does not entirely surprise me. From the point of view of the distressed person the Church appears to show little sympathy or understanding towards those whose marriages have ended in divorce. However, there are churches, and I mean the whole church community and not just the minister, who would be only too willing to offer her support or friendship. She may be wrong about her local church automatically rejecting her, though finding out might be rather painful. I think you should enquire, discreetly, for her.

I must confess that I have often felt ashamed of those churchmen who have taken a pharisaical attitude to the marriage laws, and who are more intent on preserving the edicts of *law* than of love. They claim, and no doubt believe, that they are preserving the sanctity of marriage, but to my mind a marriage that has lost its spiritual and inward grace has as little sanctity as taking communion with the lips and not the heart.

When Christ said that it was possible to commit adultery in one's heart, I think he was saying that it is not enough to keep slavishly to the outward letter of the law. The whole emphasis of Christ's teaching was on the *inner* attitude of the spirit, and not as the scribes and the pharisees would have it, on the external observance of rules. As Paul says, if you live by the law, all that the law does is condemn you. We live not by the law but by the love of Christ. The love of Christ did not condemn the woman found in adultery, but forgave her and told her to sin no more. It was to a woman who had had five husbands that he offered the living water of eternal life.

I'm afraid that many churchmen have adopted a pharisaical way of thinking. The God I worship does not condemn, but leads with love. If we hold ourselves aloof from the victims of marital breakdowns, or adulterers, then we might as well say that the Church has no room for sinners, which would be nonsense.

In the light of the leading love of God, Mrs X must not blame herelf for what has happened. Human relationships are exceedingly complex, we rarely understand ourselves, let alone our partners. For this same reason she must not hold anger or hatred in her heart towards her husband. They are both casualties and it does no good to apportion blame. You must help her to look openly and lovingly on people and the world about her. In her condition there is a great danger that bitterness and cynicism could take root, poison her mind and ultimately destroy her.

Loneliness is like an illness and it has an insidious effect on people. There is a temptation to withdraw into a shell. Fear and distrust grow within that shell, fear of being hurt, distrust of anybody's affection or love. Until you know more about her, about her strengths and weaknesses, however, it will be difficult to help her practically.

All these things are easier to say than to do, so you must pray that the loving, healing spirit of Christ will bear her up in the days to come.

Yours ever,

Spoonbill

The Manse,
Norton Woodley

Dear Mr Spoonbill,

As you know, my work in Norton Woodley includes pastoral oversight of students at Thirlbury Manor, the Teacher Training College. At the beginning of my first year I thought that an epidemic of homesickness had broken out. In the first four weeks many students were declaring that they had to go home, in some cases tearfully. I now realize that my first year was not unusual. Sadly, each year one or two students actually do go home and abandon their training.

I suppose that for many people going to college is their first experience of being away from home. Everything is so strange, the people, the institutional environment, and perhaps most importantly the freedom to study without supervision. The fact that they are no longer being treated as school children, but as adults who must work out their own study discipline, is something with which, each year, several students fail to come to terms. Of course they are neither children nor adults and naturally this in-between stage is a very disturbing time for them. Because of this, on Sundays I make the manse available to students, as a kind of second home. It took a long time to establish this, but now there are 'old hands' who make it easier for first year students.

After the morning service some students come to the manse for a lunch of the bread and cheese variety. Mrs McBride is very helpful, in fact I think she enjoys it enormously. For many of the students she's become a substitute 'mother'. I'm not old enough to be a substitute 'father' but the clerical collar does seem to enable me to say things that possibly they would not accept from either their contemporaries, or, for that matter, their real fathers. The students also come to the manse after the evening service and we've had some stimulating discussions.

I'm a little concerned about a particular student, a girl, whose constant visits to the manse and notes pushed through the door are, to say the least, a bit much. She is one of my first survivors of a homesickness crisis. On Sundays she is the first to arrive and the last to leave. Sally is amused by the attention that this girl gives me. She says that the girl is infatuated with me, but that it is no more than a 'school-girl crush' which will disappear with the arrival of her first real boyfriend. I do hope so, and the quicker her hero arrives the better.

Yours ever,

Tommy

P.S. I will enclose my essay on 'prayer' with this letter. I'm not making excuses, but if there is one thing this exercise has taught me it is that the subject of prayer cannot be encompassed in a single essay.

The Manse,
Nether Hadley

My dear Tommy,

Your work with the students sounds very positive and pastoral, as far as it goes. You make no mention of any kind of structured student society. Does your little band of Methodists do any more than attend church and chat over cheese and sandwiches?

It sounds, from your letter, as if you have taken on the role of an indulgent parent, in whose company it is forever play-time for his children. You must not try to shoulder everything yourself. There are few things more likely to deepen commitment to something than being given responsibility for it. You must channel their energies into organizing things for themselves, or perhaps helping you in your work.

Is there a properly constituted Methodist Student Society? If there is not, then I suggest that you set about founding one immediately. You must arrange for the election of a Chairman or President, a secretary and a treasurer, and perhaps invite speakers or preachers. You may be able to interest them in some local project, either in your church or community. You have clearly won their friendship, build on this. They have to grow up, you know, make their own decisions, become independent. By all means point them in the right direction, but, for their own sakes, lead from behind.

I don't want to sound like your grandmother, but you must be very careful about being alone with girls (of any age – up to at least sixty), especially those who show signs of becoming unhealthily dependent on you. Actually anybody, male or female, who begins to lean too heavily and too regularly on you, must be encouraged to stand on his own two feet.

It isn't easy. Naturally you want to help people, but it really does not help them if you become a permanent prop. You must not let visits, meetings or conversations with one person build into such a regular pattern that more significance is read into these meetings than you intend. For example, this young girl who apparently has a 'crush' on you. Don't treat it as a joke. It could be very serious. If a pattern has formed, break it. Don't be available always. Certainly, don't be alone with her. Let the students run their meetings without you occasionally.

As a minister you must be impartial. There must be a certain amount of 'detachedness' about your relationships. It may seem a bit stiff and old fashioned, but I believe it is necessary for a minister to keep a certain distance. You are the minister to a community, not to a few individuals. You must not belong to a clique. You cannot have friends who appear to be more 'special' than any other member of your church. Every member of your church must be able to think of you as their minister, not someone who is 'good with young people' or is 'in' with a particular crowd. You are minister to the young, the middle-aged and the elderly, and available to them all, equally.

You mentioned that you were able to say certain things because of your clerical collar. It is true. The clerical collar is the outward sign that you have been 'set apart'. You have been privileged to study theology, to be appointed by the Church to the pastoral care of a community of people, to share some of their most crucial experiences of sorrow and joy. You are privileged to have intimate knowledge of people's lives. The collar does set you apart. You are not 'one of the boys', you are not even you. When you speak, it is not your personal charm, however great that may be, that demands people's attention or respect, it is everything that your clerical collar represents. The Church, the Church Fathers, and the traditions and teachings of centuries. Ultimately you are a vicar of Christ, with all that implies. For all these reasons you must be careful about what you say and do. In the case of a girl with a crush on you or in the case of anyone who starts to lean on you, you must be less young Tommy Sefton-Waters, and more the Revd Thomas. Be compassionate, listen attentively, visit the sick, comfort the sorrowful; you might have to take risks sometimes but as a general rule, keep your distance from 'leaners', for their own good as well as your own.

Well Tommy, old warrior, I will let you have your 'prayer' essay back as soon as I can manage it.

God bless you,

Spoonbill

The Manse,
Norton Woodley

Dear Mr Spoonbill,

I think I've just been through one of the most difficult experiences of my life so far.

Some time ago I mentioned Edward and Marjorie Tatton. Eddy Tatton is the chap with the prize pig that made such a memorable contribution to our Harvest Festival. He and Marjorie are the tenants at Hollow Oak Farm near Woodley Park.

About a month ago (at a rather late age for

childbearing), Marjorie gave birth to a child with a heart condition; the child was not expected to live. In fact the doctor tells me that the child had also suffered brain damage and one of his limbs was malformed. He was surprised that he survived at all but he did, until last week.

Eddy and Marjorie have three boys and a daughter, all in their teens and healthy and bright – which is some consolation. I think this last child came as a great surprise to both of them. When Marjorie learned that she was pregnant, she was not at all happy about it. She thought that her childbearing days were over, and I think she resented this pregnancy, so much so that when the child was born with so many problems, she became obsessed with the idea that it was her fault and that she was being punished for not welcoming the prospect of another child.

Marjorie and Eddy have turned themselves inside out over the last month. They've had rows and screaming matches, they have wept together and talked throughout not just one night but many nights. The child, who never left hospital, brought about a crisis in their marriage. If the child had died at birth they would have shared their mutual grief as bravely as could be hoped of any couple. Because the child lived, Marjorie clung to the hope of life. Eddy however, perhaps with a farmer's realism, thought that the child would not survive and was resigned to it. It was this difference of opinion that was at the root of all their arguments, which were often exceedingly bitter.

The child was baptized in the hospital by a nurse

who, like other medical staff, did not think that he would live for much more than a few hours. He was called Peter. Marjorie was convinced with each day that passed that her life's work would be to care for this child; she began to plan on that basis, and then last Sunday the child died.

Eddy and Marjorie have discussed this terrible experience with me over several visits for hour after hour. I think she's reassured that there is no question of her being 'punished' but not surprisingly they are both very distressed.

After the funeral, Eddy asked me to go with them to Hollow Oak Farm, to have a cup of tea and a chat. They were very subdued. Marjorie seemed to be in a kind of trance, then suddenly she began shouting at me. 'What kind of a God is it that allows an innocent child to be born so deformed?' 'How can you preach about a God of love when he is so cruel?' 'What was the point of the child being born at all?' 'Why create a useless, pointless life that knew nothing but pain and death?'

I felt totally unprepared for this onslaught. What could I say? It was neither the time nor the place to give a lecture on providence or the nature of God even if I could have ordered my thoughts to do it. Her fury subsided quite suddenly and she collapsed on the sofa beside Eddy. Eddy put an arm around her and then glared at me fiercely, as if willing me to put everything right with a few well chosen words. I've never felt so inadequate in my life.

I heard myself speaking, as if I was outside the

room looking in. I was saying, 'Listen, I don't know the answer to why the innocent suffer; I don't think anybody does. I could give you all sorts of theories, but not an answer. Look, can I ask you a question?' Eddy nodded, still glaring. 'You and Eddy have been through a terrible ordeal. You have discovered things about each other, and yourselves, that you never knew. What I want to ask you is this: as a result of all this inner turmoil, the arguments and the tears, are you closer together now, or further apart?' I felt like a lawyer playing a semantic game, leading them with a question to which I already knew the answer.

There was a long silence, and then Eddy said, 'Closer, we've never been as close as we are now.' 'In which case,' I said, 'your child's life was neither pointless nor useless. If, when I die, the only thing that can be said of me is that I brought two people closer together in love, then I believe that my life will not have been wasted, and certainly Peter's life wasn't wasted. I think you're at a crossroad. You have a choice. You can let this whole experience embitter you and sour your lives, or you can let the love that Peter drew out of you grow. Do you see what I mean?' There was another long silence and then Eddy said, 'We'll think on it, Tom. We'll think on it.' I said a short prayer and then left. I felt cheap somehow. I felt as if I'd scored some sort of debating point at their expense. Somehow it was all very unsatisfactory, my contribution I mean.

* * *

It's strange how my image of the ministry has changed since I came to Norton Woodley. I sometimes saw the minister as a kind of warm-hearted father in God who went about doing good and living in a righteous glow. I couldn't have been further from the truth. Now I see that the ministry is about suffering with people, sharing their joys and trying to bring the love of God into every situation. I needed only to have reflected on Christ's ministry to have realized some of the demands, and some of the cost of ministry. I think I know now that I have a long way to go even to be worthy of attempting the task.

I've taken your advice about the students. This Sunday they'll have their first 'elections'. I've also planned my day so that apart from the services I won't be present at their meetings; I'm leaving them to get on with it. I'll keep an eye on what they get up to, but I've started to give them space to grow on their own accord. Thank you for your very helpful comments on my 'prayer' essay. I can see that I still have a lot more reading to do.

Yours ever,

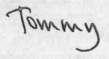

Tommy

Dear Tommy,

Well, you do seem to have dived into the deep end of the pastoral pool, but I think you have acquitted yourself splendidly. Inadequacy is a permanent state for a minister in pastoral work. We are all inadequate for this work; in fact, God help you the day you feel 'adequate'!

Whilst it is our duty to equip ourselves to the best of our ability, we can never know all the answers and it would be wrong to pretend that we do. We are, after all, only messengers, tools, instruments in the hands of the Almighty. It is never our wisdom or our strength that we offer people but always God's. If we begin to think that the salvation of those in our care is dependent on our skill as pastors and teachers then it is quite possible that our 'skill' will get in the way of the Holy Spirit. You do not have to justify God, or 'prove' God, you only have to love him and serve him. It is true some people think of ministers and priests as 'experts on God', which is, of course, nonsense. You are a servant of God. You may not understand your Lord, but you are committed to loving him and to being of what service you can. Everything you do is in and through the strength and wisdom of God. It is not your job to 'save' people, or to heal them or forgive them, you may be an instrument in any or all of these things, but it is God and God alone who saves, heals, forgives and restores.

I have made it a practice, when visiting, to say a little doorstep prayer. Before I ring the bell or knock the knocker, I remember the text, '. . . think not what you shall say in that hour, for it will not be you who speaks, but the Holy Spirit who will speak through you.' Then I add, 'Lord, be in my mind and on my lips.' Time and time again, whilst being aware of my own inadequacy, I have discovered, usually later, that the Holy Spirit is the person who has been heard speaking to people, not me.

Frequently, after preaching, people will say to you, 'Thank you so much, that sermon "spoke" to me.' If you were to question them you might well find that what they 'heard' was not actually what you said, because it is the Holy Spirit who has spoken to them. I do not mean that it doesn't matter what you say or what you do. You must use all the gifts that God has given you to the best of your ability, and God will use those gifts, but not necessarily in any way that you had imagined. Ultimately, what you *say* and what you *do* is not paramount to the person to whom you are ministering; what you *are*, is of paramount importance, and as a minister what you *are* is the instrument of the Holy Spirit.

You have committed your life to God's service. He will lead you into strange and peculiar situations, perhaps frightening situations, but if you trust in him completely you will discover that in your weakness you will find just enough strength, and in darkness, just enough light, to complete your task.

Never try to assess 'The good you have done' – that is a blind alleyway. Only God is good. Here's a useful motto for the minister: 'Duties are ours. Results are God's.' If you can follow this you will be less likely to swell with false pride, and more likely to be filled with gratitude.

God bless you,

Spoonbill

The Manse,
Norton Woodley

Dear Mr Spoonbill,

I've been trying to review the health and heart of our little community. In many ways because we are a totally rural community we have not been as hard hit by the depression as townsfolk and people in the industrial areas. I must say I don't envy Ramsay MacDonald his job. It's a curious world. A few years ago Amy Johnson flew to Australia in just nineteen days. Our scientists discovered the planet Pluto, and last Christmas the King spoke to the nation in their own homes through the wireless. Yet with all our scientific triumphs, we have nearly two and a half million people unemployed, National Hunger marches, and the humiliating 'needs test' is still with us.

In Norton Woodley, however, unemployment is nowhere near a crisis. Everyone is careful; I even know of some who are hoarding food, but most people, I think, are merely hoping that if they ignore the national situation then in time the problems will simply go away.

I must say that it's not the great crises that worry me, I mean on a pastoral level; it's not the great tragedies, suffering and death, that continually baffle me. One way and another we seem to be able to cope with these problems. No, it's the smaller things that concern me. The things that are more difficult to identify; like petty jealousies, envy, gossip, small-mindedness, meanness of spirit. These things are far more difficult to deal with. I wish I could say that they are a reflection of the economic crisis that faces the world, but I don't believe this. I think they're simply the result of the 'human' condition.

If I were able to uncover the secret thoughts of some of my church members, I fear what I might find. I suspect there's as much superstition as there is faith. I suspect that there are a few who see the whole exercise as religious insurance, 'buying their tickets' for eternity perhaps. For example, John Fielding, circuit steward, secretary of the Men's Fellowship, 'pillar of the Church'; he seems to me to have absolutely no understanding of the joy of Christian living. In fact I could describe him as a kill-joy: worthy, upright, regular in his attendance at church, but joyless. He sees wickedness in almost everything the young people want to do. Dancing, games, amusements of any kind are to him always motivated by sin and wickedness. He is laden with doom, worrying incessantly about 'what things are coming to'.

His poor wife Hetty is completely crushed by him. I can't have a conversation with her, it's always a recital of John's views, with John nodding approval, as if to a child reciting her catechism.

In a different vein, Iris Gumley is the jungle drums of the Woodley Vale circuit. There is no tittle-tattle that she doesn't know, and once she knows something her method of broadcasting her news seems more effective than the wireless. Sadly she seems to be most attentive when the news is about what she calls 'goings on'. She positively feeds on the mistakes, failures and foolishness of her neighbours. I know it sounds a hard judgement, but I can only describe her gossip as 'salacious'. On the other hand she is generous with things, if not people – gifts, jumble, food for church tea parties.

Len Castle, I'm afraid, is mean, mean to the point of being miserly. Not only with money, but with everything, mean with his time and mean with his conversation unless it's time making money or conversation about making money. I think I may have told you that Len is the hop-growing temperance man. I thought there was something strange about that combination of commitments and now I think I can understand why.

*   *   *

There are a lot of petty feuds in village life. There's always someone who isn't talking to someone else. I sometimes find myself being asked to relay messages between two people who have to do business together but are not currently on speaking terms. If someone feels that he's come off worst in a farming business exchange, the 'loser' spends months waiting to 'square things with that there rogue'. When I say there is a meanness of spirit, I mean in things like this, where people always think the worst, suspect other people's motives and brood on how they are going to 'sort things out'.

There are, thank God, notable exceptions. Henry and Clare Trevenna with their giggling daughters seem to get the best out of life. Dusty and Monica Baker are genuinely cheerful and generous people, though I have heard it said 'You have to watch Dusty. When he's grinning most, that's when he's up to a bit of clever foot-work.' Well, I don't believe there's a dishonest bone in Dusty's body. There is a difference between shrewdness and hardhearted 'doing somebody down'. I suppose I might be prejudiced. After all, Dusty is my prospective father-in-law and perhaps the glow around Sally also falls on her parents.

Mrs McBride is never happier than when she is being of service to someone. She might look fiercely at the students from time to time, but she loves them and they know it. My superintendent minister, Mr Frobisher, must have known that his gift of a housekeeper was also the gift of a right-hand friend.

Rene Fletcher, our Sunday school teacher, is the opposite side of the coin to Iris Gumley. She knows more about the real private lives of our community than Iris Gumley would be able to comprehend, but I've only ever heard her speak kindly, even of some of the more roguish locals. Sometimes when I would like information I find myself in a cleft stick – I cannot believe or even listen to Iris, and Rene would never reveal anything that she considered to be confidential knowledge. With Rene I have to read between the lines. She'll sometimes simply raise an eyebrow and say 'Really?' if I suggest something that she considers unwise or untrue. In fact I know that some of her visits to the manse are to steer me gently in the right direction, which she frequently manages to do without betraying a single confidence either by word or by implication.

All these people are upright members of the community. Some I instantly felt at home with; others don't steal, murder or molest, but at another level I find it difficult to trust them, and even more difficult to love them. It's not easy to find cracks in their armour through which the Holy Spirit might reach them. So many seem to live and die in their little internal worlds, their society within a society. I think, given the choice of ministering to a murderer or a small-minded, mealy-mouthed villager, I'd choose the murderer. I think there might be more of a chance of the murderer being able to listen.

I'm sorry if all this sounds a bit 'down' but sometimes I seem to get involved in a series of petty arguments with grown men and women behaving like children in a playground.

Forgive me, I'll try to be more cheerful next time.

Yours ever,

Tommy

> The Manse,
> Nether Hadley

Dear Thomas,

Now I wonder what it is? Lack of sleep? Indigestion? Are you 'sickening' for something? Whatever it is, your last letter sounded somewhat jaundiced. It is amazing how bad the world looks when you have an upset stomach. Perhaps you need a holiday?

Of *course* your little community is full of 'petty jealousies, envy, gossip, small-mindedness and meanness of spirit'. Its members wouldn't be human if they were not. Reading your last letter, a less generous person might be forgiven for thinking that the writer was suffering from some or all of these shortcomings. You must fight all these things in other people, and particularly in yourself, with a certain amount of humour. You must apply the humour to their stories and to yourself.

Undoubtedly a 'gossip' can do a great deal of damage, but if you take the stories seriously so will others. Take them with a pinch of salt and laugh at them. The less value you give them, the less value they will have. If the gossiper knows how little you credit the stories, it might have the effect of stopping the stories being told to you at least.

I have heard you complain before about John Fielding's 'joylessness'. It is not enough to complain, you must do something about it. You must find out what makes him so glum and censorious. You may not like him, but you must spend time getting to know him. If a doctor has an ailing patient he doesn't simply say, 'his ill health depresses me', he tries to discover the source of the ailment and then tries to relieve it. You may be able to do nothing about it, but you must at least try.

So you have a 'mean' tenant farmer. Perhaps if you had ever tried to run a small farm, feed a family and pay the rent, you might find yourself counting your pennies. Unless you have access to his accounts, how do you know that he is not actually being as generous as it is possible for him to be? Your stipend may be small, but it is not threatened by wind and storm or a long dry summer or some kind of crop disease, or any kind of crop failure.

I don't want to appear to be too hard on you, Tommy, you may be right; your farmer probably does have a mean streak, but it could be the result of generations of hardship. It is not your business to judge your people. It is your business to love them and to feed them with the nourishment of Christ.

I agree with you that the petty squabbles and feuds of a small community are very tedious and trying, but let your sense of humour lift you above them. Don't lie awake at night letting these petty feuds churn in your mind. You must set higher standards for yourself. Tonight, when you lie down if the tittle tattle of the day begins to seep into your mind, recite Dr Spoonbill's mantra:

Don't let the beggars get you down!

You can then have a good laugh, and the world will seem a little rosier in the morning.

God bless you, Tommy,

Spoonbill

The Third Year

The Manse,
Norton Woodley

Dear Mr Spoonbill,

In a previous letter I mentioned that unemployment in Norton Woodley had not reached anything like a crisis point. Which is of course a comfort only to those not actually unemployed. If there is only one person unemployed, it is a crisis for that person. Yesterday I visited Terry and Cathy Edwards who live at Overton. Terry is an unemployed carpenter and joiner. He had been with the same firm of furniture manufacturers for twenty years – a small firm in Norton St John. Two months ago they were forced to close down their factory. Terry has been unemployed since then. He had been foreman at the factory. He's now in his late fifties and sees no prospect of ever working again, certainly not in a senior position. They are surviving on their savings and what Cathy earns working in the office at the flour mill in Newton St Mary. They have one son who's married and living in Manchester.

Terry Edwards is extremely depressed. His wife Cathy tries to cheer him as best she can. She's a very outgoing person. She is in the Women's Fellowship at the Chapel, sings in the Newton St John's Ladies Choir, and frequently helps Rene Fletcher with the very small children in the Norton Woodley Sunday school. Terry used to encourage her in these activities until recently. Then I heard that Cathy had not been to the Women's Fellowship for some weeks, and Rene said that although Cathy comes to church with Terry, she no longer 'felt able' to help with the Sunday school.

Terry was out walking the dog when I called at their house. Which was fortunate in a way, because it meant that I could talk with Cathy on her own. She thought I'd come to ask why she had stopped attending the Women's Fellowship and helping out in the Sunday school. I hadn't, but nevertheless she told me: 'He's getting very jealous of the things I do', she said. 'Now that he's at home all the time he resents my going out to things, especially as I'm out working all day. So I've given everything up except my job – we depend on it so much now. But Terry even resents that.'

She told me that there had been a vacancy for a labourer at the Flour Mill and she had tried to persuade him to apply for that job as a temporary measure. At first he objected. 'I'm a craftsman, not a so-and-so labourer.' Eventually she won him round and he got the job, but he only worked there for one day.

On the day he started she had hurried home to get his tea ready, but to her surprise, he was already there.

'I don't want to talk about it,' he said. 'It's not for me, that's all.' Cathy didn't know what happened until the next day. When she got to the office, it was the one topic of conversation.

It seems that there is a young foreman in charge of the labourers at the mill, less than half Terry's age. Apparently this chap had kept calling Terry 'Grandad' and telling him he'd have to 'put his back into it' if he wanted to keep the job. Eventually he threw one taunt too many and Terry had picked up a sack of flour (he's a big chap), held it above his head and then heaved it at the foreman. It had sent him flying.

Terry had ripped off his miller's apron and thrown that at the foreman, saying, 'One day, sunny Jim, you'll be my age, you'll be out of work and you'll remember this day. See if you don't.' With that he had marched off home. He's now more convinced than ever that he could not face working under some 'jumped up pip-squeak', and that it's extremely unlikely that he'll get a job suitable to his age and experience.

Cathy says that he has had some wild ideas about going to Bristol and setting up his own business. Sometimes he talks about emigrating to Canada or Australia. Cathy thinks he's too old to start again, and anyway she doesn't think she could face such a big move at her age.

When Terry arrived home the conversation became a bit stilted, so after we'd had a cup of tea I excused myself and left. Heaven knows what they do in the evenings. She has given up all her interests and he doesn't appear to have any.

I don't know how much contact you have with the unemployed in Nether Hadley, but if you have any thoughts on the matter I would be very grateful.

Yours ever,

Tommy

The Manse,
Nether Hadley

Dear Tommy,

I'm afraid your story about the unemployed carpenter is all too familiar to me. He is in the comparatively early stages of his unemployment; if you are to help him it must be soon. The longer his unemployment lasts the more likely he is to withdraw into himself. He has suffered a terrible blow to his pride, to his concept of himself as a man, as a husband and as a 'provider'. To such a man the fact that he is dependent on his wife's earnings only increases his sense of frustration.

One of the difficulties for somebody in his position is that in time depression takes hold of the will to fight back. It drains people of energy; mental, physical and spiritual. They find it hard to pray. What has to be done is a real appraisal of the situation, a coming to terms with things as they really are. It is pointless talking about 'what used to be'. He must face up to where he is now. He must examine his talents and abilities and see how he might use them to earn a living. So then, what can he do?

You say that he has had some 'wild ideas'. What's wrong with that? They should be encouraged and followed through until they collapse as unrealistic. Perhaps they won't collapse. Don't forget that 'dream' can be another word for 'hope', and that is what you must keep alive.

Out of the ashes of his previous career might arise a whole new way of life. That is really what he should be looking for now, not a career, but a satisfying way of life. He must not expect position and status and a senior rate of pay. He might achieve all those things, but that should not be the aim. His aim should be, 'What can I do that will make my life worthwhile, for me and my wife?' If he wants to start a business in Bristol, discuss it with him. If he wants to emigrate, discuss that with him. Incidentally, if you have need of a carpenter to put something right on your church premises, then get it done now, and be certain that the church pays the rate for the job.

His wife, Cathy, is clearly willing to help in any way she can. I'm not sure that giving up all her activities was necessarily the best thing to do. There is a danger that they will both sit and mope together. The more 'alive' their household is, the better; it won't be easy for her, but she must not let him sink into self-pity. When you next see him make sure you have done your homework. Find out about emigration and if there is any need abroad for his craft, at his age. You can then talk intelligently about one of the wild dreams.

Of course you will pray for them, but, old warrior, you are in touch with far more people than he is, so, in addition to raising your voice in prayer, keep your ear to the ground. You never know what might turn up.

God bless you,

Spoonbill

**The Manse,
Norton Woodley**

Dear Mr Spoonbill,

I had no sooner read your letter than who should knock at my door but Mrs Driver's son-in-law. Mrs Driver is the baker's widow. Her husband died after asking me to 'lay hands' on him. Do you remember? Mrs Driver's son-in-law, William, is a gardener at Thirlbury Teacher Training College. For over a year now he has had *two* jobs, one as a gardener. In his spare time, in the evenings, he has been helping Mrs Driver in the bakery. I don't know when he slept! Mrs Driver's daugher Frances has been running the shop as well as she could whilst coping with two small children. Mrs Driver, who for the last year found it very difficult to do anything, seems now to have come through some kind of barrier and has started to work in the shop again.

William had called on me for advice. He felt he could no longer continue to help out at the bakery, and was at the end of his tether. His wife, Frances, feels that she has been neglecting her children. In short, they wanted to break away completely from the bakery, but how could they do it without hurting Mrs Driver? Whilst we were talking about this, the doorbell rings yet again and who is on the door step but Terry and Cathy Edwards. Cathy had persuaded Terry to come and see me on the grounds that, I quote, 'the minister knows a lot of people and might be able to help.'

To use the word 'miraculous' might be going too far, but it was the most extraordinary set of coincidental circumstances I have yet experienced.

To be brief: as you have probably guessed by now, after a suitable period of handing-over-training from William, and further continuing training from Mrs Driver, the new full-time baker in Norton Woodley will be Mr Terence Edwards.

William is convinced that if he had suggested the idea to his mother-in-law, she would have rejected it, but as the idea apparently came from me, and as Mrs

Driver cannot be dissuaded from the idea that since I laid hands on her husband everything I say is 'divinely inspired', she agreed at once.

Further, Terry won't be an employee, but a partner. He's investing the remains of his savings in the bakery, which has been run in a somewhat, forgive me, 'half-baked' manner, and is in need of some revitalization. Terry, with all his furniture making, carpentry and joinery skills, intends to redesign and rebuild the shop interior. In a very short time the legend, 'Driver and Edwards, Bakers', will appear over the window of the bakery. Terry is a new man. Cathy will be singing in the Newton St John's production of *The Messiah* this year. Mrs Driver has made a generous gift to the church, in spite of my cautionary advice to wait and see how things turn out.

Frances and William, with sighs of relief, have returned to their children and the peace of Thirlbury Manor gardens.

I only hope that everything does work out, or Mrs Driver's faith in me will be shattered!

Yours, amazed,

Tommy

The Manse,
Nether Hadley

Dear Tommy,

As you and I would agree that the carpenter and the baker's widow saga involves an extraordinary series of coincidences, I hesitate to say 'Well done', but 'Well done' anyway.

Whilst we should hesitate to attribute every coincidence to the activity of the Holy Spirit, one of the things that you will notice over the years is that 'coincidences' seem to abound in the life of a minister. Time and time again I have found myself on the doorstep of somebody's home, having called on a sudden impulse, only to be greeted with, 'Oh, Mr Spoonbill, how did you know?' In fact, it happens so frequently that I have stopped thinking of these incidents as 'coincidence'. I have stopped trying to work out what possible series of facts or signs have resulted in my taking some kind of 'intuitive' action. I find myself saying, 'There are more things in heaven and earth, Horatio, than are dreamt of in your philosophy'. So saying, I then simply offer a prayer of thanksgiving.

Thomas, you are now in your third year as a probationer. I have no doubt whatsoever that you will be of great service to the Church and to the communities in which you will serve. I have been thinking about your forthcoming marriage.

There is no 'probationary' period in marriage, apart from courtship. Once embarked upon, the commitment is total from the word 'go'. As I look back over the years of my own marriage, and reflect on all the married couples I have known, a number of observations spring to mind. For what they are worth, and I hope you do not think me impertinent, I would like to share some of these thoughts with you.

The marriage of a minister and his wife has certain advantages, but there are also certain disadvantages. One of the advantages is that usually you share your working life together in a way which few other couples can. Your mutual headquarters is the manse, your home. You are involved together in all the meetings that happen at the manse. The callers at the door have come not merely to your office but to your home.

Some people may feel that they can confide in your wife more easily than they can in you. In the ordinary way a wife will hear about, and perhaps meet, some of her husband's colleagues, but a minister's wife will know all the people that you work with, and sometimes she will know them better than you do. It is a shared ministry, a shared life and that is a great privilege and blessing. You are more likely to know how your partner is feeling. A great deal of marriage is sharing, and in the ministry you start off with a very definite advantage in this area.

The disadvantage of all this is that so much of your life together is invaded by the demands of the ministry. Because your home is your headquarters, it is difficult to enjoy any privacy. The few evenings that you have at home, rather than at some church meeting, will be broken into. Meals are interrupted. People come and don't know when to leave. You can be disturbed in the middle of the night. Whilst both of you may be prepared for this, you will have to plan some regular form of escape. You must have some life which is yours and yours alone.

It is traditional for ministers to take Mondays as their day off. Unfortunately crises occur on Mondays as often as they do on any other day of the week, so it is a difficult rule to keep. If people are in distress you can't say, 'I'm sorry, it's my day off'. But as far as you are able, you must try to keep at least one day as your own.

There are some things that cannot be shared. If somebody makes a confession to you, shares the most intimate secrets of their lives with you, then you are morally bound to keep these things secret. Sometimes people may test your trustworthiness. My wife has told me of a number of occasions when people have called and said something like, 'Oh, I expect Mr Spoonbill has told you about my problem'.

If people suspect that you might discuss their problems with your wife, they will, of course, cease to trust you as their pastor. So you must make it very clear to people that if they wish to confide in you, you will respect that confidence absolutely. There will be many nights when you will lay your head on your pillow with your mind full of things that you can only share with your Maker.

Apart from the pastoral confessions, there must be no secrets between you and your wife. It is better to have a heated discussion than to nurse things in silence. There are few things more likely to cause a mutual rift than undiscussed problems; secret anger is a canker in the soul. A hurt nursed in silence will grow and become distorted. A fundamental rule of marriage is – face up to things together. When the talking, or even the rowing, stops, a marriage comes under severe strain. It is a denial of the very word 'marriage'.

A good marriage is a continual voyage of discovery. You ought never to reach the position where you feel that you know all there is to know about each other. It will never be true anyway. The people we are in our twenties, are not the same people in their forties, or sixties. Time, experience, circumstances, health, all these things change us. We are new people every day. To grow together in mutual understanding and love is perhaps the most difficult task we can ever face. Marriage is not something which happens one day in a church, it is a lifetime's work. It is 'working' at a marriage that so many people tire of quickly. 'They lived happily ever after' must be one of the most misleading phrases ever coined. 'And they *worked* at living happily ever after' might be more helpful.

A marriage in a rut is one of the saddest and most dispiriting things to meet. Unfortunately you will come across such marriages many times. I am not talking about unfaithful partners or that kind of thing, I'm talking about apathy and inertia. I mean those marriages where both people have ceased to work at their marriage and have sunk into a kind of dull-eyed acceptance. They have become marriages that are outwardly and physically in existence, but are inwardly and spiritually dead, or at least comatose. If you 'give up' over one area of your marriage, that is, reach the point when you say, 'Oh well, he, or she, will never change, so I'm not going to bother any more', you have reached the beginning of the end. You may end up not so much running away from each other as drifting apart in apathy.

Sometimes people who have been divorced will come to you, asking to be married again to a new partner. It is your duty to help such a person to face up to where their marriage went wrong, in particular, where *they* went wrong. Unless they come to terms with what happened in their previous marriage then the likelihood is that their next marriage will founder on similar rocks, or on the same inability to recognize problems and deal with them.

So often people do not listen to each other. They talk, but they are only listening to themselves, and thinking about what they are going to say next rather than listening to what their partner is saying at that moment. And, oh dear! What things we do say!

For instance, issuing ultimatums, which is never a good thing. 'That's the *last* time I will *ever*. . . .' It isn't, and you will. 'If you *ever* do that again. . . .' They will do it again. If you issue an ultimatum to yourself, you are unlikely to keep it. 'I will *never*, *ever*, say porridge again! Because porridge –', whoops! If you cannot keep to your own ultimatums, why should you expect other people to keep to ultimatums that you issue to them? You are not perfect. Don't expect your partner to be.

I suppose in any conflict of opinion it is always difficult to admit a mistake, or an error of judgement, or a hasty word. It is extremely difficult, and requires great maturity, to be able to say, 'I'm sorry, I was wrong', or, 'I'm sorry, that was my fault', or 'I'm sorry, that was a stupid thing to say'.

Again, never be reluctant to accept an apology. It takes great effort to apologize, always recognize it. Don't forgive conditionally. If God were to lay down conditions for our forgiveness, we would be lost. Our redemption depends on the freely given forgiveness of God. Who are we to lay down conditions for others to win our forgiveness?

There is a good motto that should be shared by married couples, and it is this:

'Never let the sun set on your wrath.' Or in other words, 'Never go to bed in a temper with each other.'

I hope I'm not painting too dismal a prospect for you. I'm just trying to think of the pitfalls. There will be so many moments of sheer joy; shared laughter, family meals, Christmas holidays, games, evenings around the fire, shared adventures and shared sorrows that will build up a loving, trusting relationship, that no disagreement should ever be allowed to destroy. It takes a lot of effort to build a marriage, there will be tears and much agonizing, but it's worth it. There is no other relationship that can compare with it. People point to failed, miserable, intolerable marriages and argue for some other kind of relationship. To me, that is like pointing at some diseased rose and arguing for the abolition of roses.

Everything I have said so far applies to atheist, agnostic or believer. Where there is a bond of faith, there is, I am convinced, a far greater chance of marital success. A couple who have called on God to unite them have embarked on a different journey from those who have called only on the law of the land to unite them. The law is indifferent, God is not. The law is a legal framework, outside and around your marriage. God works from within. A marriage in law is between two people, witnessed by the state. In holy matrimony man and woman are joined by the continuing presence of the Holy Spirit. The husband and wife who pray together, worship together, consecrate their children in baptism and in the name of God who joined them in marriage, are never alone in their adventure.

The Christian marriage is one that is lived in the knowledge of the continuing presence of God. If their faith is not merely lip-service, but a true commitment to the God of love, a real awareness of the sacrificial love of Christ, a genuine desire for the Holy Spirit to guide their lives, then they have an immeasurable advantage in their mutual task of growing together in love.

The fact that the Christian marriage is, by its very nature, a unit within a larger family, means that such a marriage should never be isolated or inward looking. Christ taught that to find life is to die to self, and that to die to yourself is to find real life. A marriage based on this teaching is a marriage that will grow in love. While it is necessary to know and understand each other, and to go on learning about each other, it is also necessary for the Christian marriage to look outwards, to find ways of serving God in the community and the world at large. The greater their concern to serve Christ, the greater their desire to find opportunities of sharing the love of Christ, the more likely it will be that their marriage will meet every trial in the strength of Christ.

We are all human. We all get tired, and ill-tempered. We all sin, against God and each other, but through Christ we are aware of the forgiving nature of God and of his untiring love. Because of this we will try to be no less forgiving and loving to the

·one to whom, in the name of Christ, we have been united in marriage.

Well, Thomas, I think I have been meandering around and through an enormous subject. No one can point to the perfect marriage, but every married couple can reach out to the perfect love that has been revealed to us in Christ, and in the light of that there is hope for us all.

God bless you,

Spoonbill

The Manse,
Norton Woodley

Dear Mr Spoonbill,
Last Saturday I spent a day with the students in 'retreat' at Woodley Park chapel. It was entirely at their request. They wanted to spend a day, thinking and praying, under my guidance. They had chosen as their theme the question, 'Where are we going?' As I'm constantly asking myself that question, I was happy to oblige. Sally was free that weekend so she came with us. I don't know who was helped most, the students, or Sally and me. It certainly helped me.

We started off with a discussion of the question,

'Where are we going?' I suggested that it might be useful if we spent an hour privately and silently, asking ourselves, 'What is it I want out of life?' I thought it would be a good thing if we all faced up to this question as honestly as possible, trying to isolate what we really want from what we have been taught or conditioned to think we *ought* to want. I assured them that no one would ask them what conclusions they reached. Their thoughts would remain entirely private.

After a short period of prayer together we separated as best we could. There are a number of rooms or areas at Woodley Park chapel, a vestry, two schoolrooms, the chapel itself, the vestibule and a fairly large kitchen. We distributed ourselves around these spaces; some people chose to go out and walk, either down the lane or across the fields.

I thought that some students might find it difficult to cope with silence. I remembered from my student days that on similar retreats, watching my friends solemnly trying to keep silence, was inclined to induce an embarrassing desire to giggle. So I suggested that anyone who felt that this exercise might be too difficult could either go for a walk on their own or find a corner and read a book.

An hour later, when we gathered together after a cup of tea, I posed the next question: 'How can we achieve our aims?' If our 'aim' was something that we really wanted to do above all else, then, I suggested, whatever we had to do, and no matter how long it took, if we kept that aim in view we would be likely to achieve it. Our natural talents and leanings would no doubt have influenced our 'aim', and therefore probably, despite snags and difficulties, our 'aim' could be achieved. So our next quiet period would be spent examining the questions, 'How do I achieve my aims?', 'What are the difficulties?' and 'How can I overcome them?'

I then read from the first letter of Paul to the Corinthians (chapter 12), 'Now there are diversities of gifts. . . ' Again, after a short prayer, we went our separate ways.

I must confess that although, as an ordinand, I know beyond doubt that I want to serve God, as a minister, when I ask myself, 'What do I *really* want?' the answer seems to be, 'Adventure, and adventure shared with someone I love.'

I know that when I was interviewed by the Missionary Society I gave what I hoped would be thought high-minded reasons for wanting to serve overseas. I didn't say that my principal reason was a simple desire for adventure. I'm beginning to think that I was deceitful, although I'm not sure if at that time I really knew what my real motives were.

I seem to have gone a long way towards achieving my aim. This time next year will probably find me married and living in 'foreign parts'. Sally seems to have been heaven-sent. She shares so many of my hopes and dreams.

After a picnic lunch we talked about our aims in general terms, rather than in particular detail. Our group shared the following common desires:

We want to be useful.
We want to be needed.
We want to love and be loved.

Our final question, for private thought and prayer, was 'What do our hopes and aims look like in the light of the love of God, as revealed in Jesus Christ?'

In general discussion after tea we concluded that most of us felt that some of our hopes and aims, in the light of Christ, seemed trivial or selfish. I then raised the question, 'What did Jesus mean when he said, that the greatest commandments were, "to love God, and our neighbour as ourselves".' I raised this because there seemed to be a feeling that unless we were sacrificial in our lives then our lives might be worthless. Whilst this may have a great deal of truth in it, it seemed to me that this thought was being linked with a rather mistaken idea that it was therefore selfish to spend your life doing something that gave you pleasure. There was a tendency to wallow in guilt. Some students seemed to be saying that because so many people in the world are suffering from hunger and poverty, we should not enjoy our comparative wealth. Mr Spoonbill, does this mean that eating should not be a pleasure? There is never a time when there is nobody suffering or dying, does this mean we should never laugh? Surely we should celebrate and enjoy every blessing. We should express our gratitude to a generous God in enjoyment. Our guilty feelings don't relieve suffering.

It was for all these reasons that I wanted to discuss the phrase 'to love God, and our neighbour as ourselves'. I remember being told about a sermon in which a very distinguished theologian said that you cannot love your neighbour, or even know what love means, if you don't love yourself. Jesus didn't say 'Love your neighbour *instead* of yourself.' I should think that it is equally true that if we cannot forgive ourselves then we will not be able to forgive others either.

The discussion was lively and thoughtful. We closed the day with Communion in the chapel. It was a beautiful act of worship. Every part of it seemed to have been heightened by the intensity of prayer and thought that had preceded it.

I think that our retreat helped to clarify our thoughts. Perhaps we all began to see what things really matter, and perhaps we also began to be realistic about ourselves and our gifts. I'm glad also that in our discussions we laughed a lot. I think real freedom is being able to laugh at yourself and your own pretensions. If nothing else the retreat has certainly deepened our fellowship.

Best wishes,

Tommy

> *The Manse,*
> *Nether Hadley*

Dear Tommy,

I wish I had been able to attend your retreat. I think you will find that the question 'Where am I going?' does not disappear with age. I shouldn't worry or feel guilty about the realization that you want some adventure in your life. You will not have deceived the Missionary Society; they will have recognized your desire for adventure without your having to confess to it. What is wrong with a desire for adventure anyway? The whole of the Christian life is an adventure in faith.

I must confess to you that it seems like only yesterday when I stood in your place and wondered about the future. But it is not a misty memory of years ago. I still have hopes and dreams. So what can I advise you or your students? I think you can tell them from me that life is a continuous exploration, a search for the dream. Life is not a job, or a qualification, or a particular success, but a series of discoveries.

You can tell them that when they are in their seventies or eighties, they will still be on the nursery slopes of discovery. The excitement of being alive is not merely arriving at destinations, or achieving goals. It is the journey itself which is exciting. Whilst one day's retreat may be a great stimulus, they have not arrived; God protect them if they ever do feel that they have. You must convey to them my conviction that they must never stop searching. If they do, they will have stopped living.

You mentioned, almost in passing, the importance of being able to forgive ourselves. Forgiveness mends the person, but not necessarily the sin. If, in a fit of temper, I break something, forgiveness will heal me, but not mend what is broken. We have to find ways, if it is possible, to make restitution.

The fact remains that it is more difficult to forgive ourselves than it is to forgive others, possibly because we are rather inclined to take ourselves too seriously. This is where your sense of humour has to come to the rescue. We may find ourselves chuckling at the mistakes and foibles of others, but we do find it difficult to laugh at our own stupidities, we are far too egocentric. There is even the danger of clinging to our mistakes, or perhaps sporting them like medals; in other words, we have a tendency to wallow in our self-inflicted misery because of a mistaken sense of our own importance.

If we develop, perhaps as a kind of self-discipline, a tight-lipped attitude towards ourselves, then it will make generosity and forgiveness towards others far more difficult.

Forgive us our sins, as we forgive those who sin against us.

'Forgive us our sins' should be addressed to our Heavenly Father, but it should also be addressed to ourselves.

My dear Thomas, you seem to be making great strides with the students.

Battle on, old warrior!

God bless you,

Spoonbill

The Manse,
Norton Woodley

Dear Mr Spoonbill,

Last Tuesday evening John Fielding called at the manse to recite one of his regular litanies of faults in chapel and community. His complaints can be about almost anything, acts of worship, a visiting preacher's sermon, chapel committees, trustees' meetings, young people, the community at large and especially his farming brethren. His criticism of me is usually implied rather than direct, but nevertheless he makes his disapproval known! I cannot deny that some of his complaints are valid, but some are rather petty.

It suddenly occurred to me that this was a good opportunity to clear the air, or at least to try to. It was one of the few times I'd been with him alone. I decided to take the bull by the horns and speak to him openly about himself. In nearly three years of looking at that tight-lipped face, I couldn't remember seeing him smile, ever. I doubt if I had heard one word of encouragement, or, for that matter, heard him speak well of anyone.

When he had finished his complaints list, which he keeps in a little note-book, I asked him as quietly and deliberately as I could: 'John, what's the matter with you? I mean *really* the matter?'

I don't know how I expected him to answer me. I suppose I thought that he would prevaricate, or get angry. For a moment he glared at me, his great black eyebrows drawn into a straight line. To my astonishment, he closed his eyes and let out an enormously deep sigh, it was almost a groan. I didn't know what to think. I wondered if he was going to hurl himself at the door, or even at me. Then he suddenly relaxed and sank back into his arm chair, his head flopping back so that, for what seemed like eternity, I was left studying the blue-black bristles under his chin. When he spoke, his voice startled me.

'It's a long story. Do you really want to hear it?'

It was a strangely dramatic moment. I had to swallow before I could speak. I assured him that I did want to hear, and that he could take as long as he liked.

Listening, I began to understand a little better the changes that have occurred in the last fifty years. John Fielding was born in 1880, in a world that no longer exists. The man he always thought of as his father was a seaman. He never knew him. Everything he knew about this man had been related to him by his mother. She had told him heroic stories in which his father had always triumphed over sea and storm. He had survived shipwreck and attacks from savages, but ultimately, in the Southern Ocean, whilst bound for Australia, he had died in an attempt to save a drowning shipmate in a violent storm.

It was only as Fielding grew older that he began to realize the inconsistencies in his mother's stories. Only as a young boy did he realize that the 'uncles' who called on his mother were not uncles, and that his mother was not a 'brave widow', but a member of the oldest profession.

As soon as he was able, he left Bristol and looked for work in the country. He never wanted to see a sailor or hear the sea. He wanted to shake the dust of Bristol from his feet, to erase his past and create a new life for himself.

He ended up in Herefordshire, working for a farmer who virtually adopted him as a son. He was happy for a few years, until the farmer discovered that his daughter was in love with Fielding. The farmer, who had ambitions for his daughter, turned Fielding out, but not until they had come to blows. Fielding believes that he must have caused the farmer internal injury, because less than a month later the farmer died. The farmer's daughter, who had inherited her father's farm, made enquiries as to Fielding's whereabouts and found him. She assured him that her father had died naturally, but he didn't believe her. He returned to the farm and a year later they were married. Within the next year his wife died in childbirth. It was then that Fielding became convinced that he was waging a personal war with the devil.

He believes that he has a personal devil who has pursued him all his life. When he married his present wife, Hetty, he selected her because she was simple-minded, shy, submissive and an orphan like himself. He did not tell her about his devil when she lost her first and only child, also in childbirth. Shortly after this tragedy he sold the farm and moved to Woodley Vale.

Since then he has fought the devil by not giving him an inch. He has put up barriers against every conceivable weakness in his defence. He has fought the devil with iron discipline. The devil still tries to get him. Every blighted crop is the work of the devil. Every sick animal is demon-possessed. He confessed that when Eddy Tutton's pig had disrupted the Harvest Festival he was convinced that the devil had been trying to reach him through the animal. I realize now that Fielding's outburst after the Harvest service was not motivated by righteous anger, but by fear.

It is true that these are difficult times, economically, for everyone, but Fielding does seem to have had more than his share of bad luck. He listed all the farming enterprises that had gone wrong for him. A lesser man might have quit before now, but because of his iron will he has clawed his way through crisis after crisis.

His litany of complaints is all part of his battle against evil and the devil. Every piece of slackness, on anyone's part, he sees as a possible opportunity for the devil to get a finger-hold into some aspect of his life. So for years he has rapped the devil's knuckles at every opportunity.

This attempt to keep the devil at bay can be seen in everything he does: the way he conducts himself at meetings, even the way he decorates his house. Everything in his house is white, every wall, every window, every door. 'The devil can't stand white, you know.' His house is also like a fortress. Every door has bolts and locks, every window is shuttered, and he is obsessed with building walls. Which makes sense when you realize that he has been under siege for years.

As I listened to him I began to wonder if he was mad. He is utterly convinced of his life-long personal battle with the devil. He's continually on guard against the possibility of the devil slipping through his defences. I now see that his severe, pinched and lined face is the face of a persecuted man, whether the persecution is fact or fantasy.

I asked him about his belief in God. He told me quite

openly that he did not love God, but feared him. He knew that he was being punished because of his mother. 'All of this is the result of that evil woman's life.' 'It's her fault that I suffer as I do.' 'You see, when I left home, it was her devil who followed me.' He is also being punished because of the death of his first wife's father, whom he believes died because of him. He said that he hoped to love God one day, when he had paid the penalty for his mother's sins, 'Though I doubt if I will achieve that this side of the grave.'

I asked him about the prayers we had shared together, thanking God for his love, he replied, 'You might know the love of God, but I don't.' I said, 'What about communion? You attend communion regularly. What does that mean to you?' 'Safety', he said, 'I wish we had communion more often. I always feel safe after communion.'

I tried to talk to him about the love of God and the forgiveness of God, but I felt as if I was talking to a blank wall. At least there was a benefit for John Fielding – he has shared his problem with someone else. He was most concerned that I should not discuss it with his wife. 'She's an innocent you know. It would only upset her.'

Well, Mr Spoonbill, I hardly know where to begin – whether I should advise him to see a specialist doctor, or simply try to guide him myself, though I hardly feel qualified to do that. What do you think?

Yours ever,

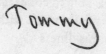
Tommy

Dear Tommy,

I am so glad that you have at last tackled the problem of John Fielding. I have had a feeling in my bones that the poor fellow was deeply troubled about something.

I do not know if, at your college, the curriculum included any study of psychology, probably not, though I am more and more convinced that a working knowledge of this developing science will be an essential part of a minister's training in the future.

In many ways ministers have always been psychologists. As you know 'psyche' comes from the Greek word for 'breath' or 'soul', and therefore psychology is really the study of the soul or mind. As a science the subject is, comparatively, in its infancy. It is treated by some people with a certain degree of scepticism. Nevertheless, I am convinced that we have a great deal to learn about the influence of the mind on behaviour and health generally.

From what little I have read on the subject, the word 'paranoia' seems to fit John Fielding's condition. Paranoia is an illness which is characterized by either delusions of grandeur or persecution, or perhaps both, by someone who in other aspects of his life has an apparently untroubled mind and therefore, for the most part, is able to conceal his paranoia. He is able to go about his daily work without people knowing anything about his illness.

The difficulty you face is that the delusions of persecution may stem from a reasonable and perhaps logical premise. Things do seem to have followed a dreadful pattern in his life and it will therefore be difficult to persuade him to reinterpret those events and re-evaluate his life.

I often wonder if people unconsciously co-operate with disaster. That is to say, expecting the worst to happen, they somehow contribute to the disaster. Conversely, I wonder if the happy-go-lucky person, by his attitude, unconsciously resists disaster and by his positive frame of mind contributes towards his own 'good fortune'. It seems to be a trick of the mind, which perhaps could be learned and developed, unless the pessimism is endogenous, that is, has its roots in a physical condition.

In Fielding's case we do not have to look far for 'causes' of his illness. They seem to be clear from his account of his life, although it is possible that you have not yet heard the full story, but if we have correctly identified the illness and are acquainted with the possible cause, the question that remains is, 'What is the treatment?' At the moment there are very few opportunities for the long-term therapeutic treatment that Fielding needs. You may not feel qualified, but in the heart of rural Herefordshire, I think, as his pastor, you will have to shoulder the burden.

You have, of course, started his treatment by the simple expedient of asking him, 'What is the matter?' You may feel that you have done very little, but that question led him to a major decision, the decision to confide in you, which he seems to have done without restraint. You may never learn why, after all these years, he chose to tell you. It may be that you are the first person to give him the opportunity.

You have made a good start, but in his case the therapy may well be more complicated than simply listening, and may take many hours of constructive attention and talk. Now that you have begun, you must, for his sake, continue. You must see him regularly. Whilst offering him understanding, reassurance, support and guidance, you are actually embarking on a very complicated exercise. You are seeking, ultimately, to bring about a definite and permanent change in his personality. Somehow you have to make him aware of his delusion, and help him to alter his whole pattern of thought, so that his attitude to life is changed for the better. Your aim is to help him to become a happier man. It is not likely to happen overnight.

Success will depend a great deal upon a good working relationship. He must trust you to help him with tact and yet absolute honesty. Most of all he must be aware of your professional detachment. If you become emotionally involved you will not be able to make sound or clear-sighted judgements. This applies to all pastoral relationships. The fact that you have found it difficult to like this man may well be in your favour. If he was a close friend I would have recommended somebody else to help him. He must not simply lean on you for support, you must be the means by which his awareness of the real nature of his problems is increased. You must be the means of his discovering his *own* methods of dealing with his condition.

If you show neither distress nor hostility towards his confessions, if he knows you to be somebody who both understands and accepts him, and I think you may have already achieved this, then you will have given him a new lease of life.

If you feel perplexed about Fielding's physical health, then you might have to consult a physician, or persuade him to see a doctor. Whatever you do, don't rush him, don't frighten him off.

I must warn you that the deeper you go into Fielding's state of mind, the greater is the possibility that he will become hostile towards you. The anger that he feels towards, say, his mother, might be released on you. You will have to control the progress of his self-discovery so that he can see what he is doing, what is happening within himself. In the end you will have to rely on your own natural ability, skill and judgement in dealing with people. There is a possibility that it could go wrong, but in the circumstances I do not see what choice you have in the matter.

I have one or two books on the subject of psycho-analysis. I'll parcel them up and send them to you.

Tread carefully Tommy. I will pray for you,
God bless you,

Spoonbill

Dear Mr Spoonbill,

Thank you for the books. At college we were introduced to the subject of psychology in our Pastoral Theology lectures. At the time they were of mild academic interest. I didn't then realize how important the subject really is. I think I shall be consulting your letter frequently. I saw Fielding in Norton Woodley and he's going to call on me again next Tuesday. It may have been my imagination but he seemed to have more of a spring in his step. His attitude to me has changed markedly. He was quite conspiratorial, which I took as a good sign. Whatever he is fighting, I think he feels that he is no longer alone in the battle.

It is amazing the things that happen during a short walk down the High Street. After talking to John Fielding I looked in at the bakery, which Terry Edwards has already transformed. Mrs Driver is looking more her old self, she's definitely back in harness. She is actually a very shrewd business woman, despite the fact that she becomes strangely and rather embarrassingly coy in my presence. I left the bakery clutching an ovenwarm cottage loaf which she insisted on giving to me.

Iris Gumley was rattling away to Monica Barker, nineteen to the dozen, outside Norton Woodley's one and only dress shop. I stopped to say hello and Iris blushed to the roots of her hair, so heaven knows what she had been prattling about.

Outside 'Fletcher, Swanley and Son, Solicitors', I met Rene Fletcher talking to George Swanley, the 'son' in Fletcher, Swanley and Son. After a few pleasantries Rene hurried off about her shopping, leaving me to have a most extraordinary conversation with George Swanley. At least it seemed to me to be extraordinary to be standing in Norton Woodley High Street discussing belief in God. George Swanley must clearly have been thinking about it for some time, or perhaps it is just the effect the clerical collar has on people.

I doubt if my walk down the High Street took much more than thirty minutes, but in that time I had a conversation with a farmer, received a gift from the bakery, engendered a touch of conscience in a gossip and started a theological discussion with an agnostic solicitor. Whatever else village life is, it's certainly not boring, certainly not for a parson.

George Swanley had to hurry off to the county sessions in Hereford that morning, but we arranged to have tea at the manse the following afternoon. It was an interesting encounter.

I suspect that, like many people, George Swanley's religious thinking ceased the day he last attended Sunday school. It seems to me, from conversations I've had with students and lecturers, as well as from my conversation with George, that the childlike concepts of God as taught in the Sunday school are rarely developed. In fact they are usually rejected, as time goes by, as 'charming fairy stories for children', or as 'unrealistic' in the light of the modern world.

If people don't conceive of God as an old man with a flowing white beard, sitting in the clouds, their concept is not far removed from this. Obviously I'm making a sweeping generalization, but I think there is an element of truth in what I'm saying.

George Swanley, again like many others, despite the rejection of his Sunday school God, has a nagging feeling that, 'there might be something in it'. After all, some extremely intelligent people seem to have staked their lives on it. 'To be perfectly honest,' he said, 'I wish I *could* believe in God.'

It's so difficult to know where to start in such a conversation. There are so many classic arguments for the existence of God, but most of them are based on a philosophical argument that requires some knowledge of logic as a technical system of reasoning. For most people I think their belief in God is based on personal experience, that is, they 'know' God rather than 'prove' him. Sally once said to me, when I was arguing with a student, 'All I know is that when I worship or pray, my life works better than when I don't.' Or in other words, God is reality in her life and 'proving his existence' is simply not necessary.

I decided to start with George's initial statement: 'I wish I could believe in God.' I assured him that if this was really true, that he sincerely wanted to believe in God, then he was already halfway there. I told him about Pascal's statement, 'To seek God is to find him.' However, I added that although this was true, it implied an 'active' seeking after God rather than an occasional vague thought: 'Wouldn't it be nice if there was a God.' George then asked, 'How do I "actively" seek God?'

I suggested that 'seeking God' was not something that you could confine to rainy afternoons. It's not merely an academic exercise, however fascinating or absorbing, but involves a total commitment to a spiritual adventure. After all, how could you be anything less than totally committed when you are pursuing ultimate things, ultimate questions, such as 'Who am I?', 'What do I exist for?', 'Where am I going?', 'Is there any meaning to life?', 'Is death the end?' The answers to these questions must surely dictate how we live our lives, and therefore they cannot be taken lightly.

I felt it best that, rather than embark on a philosophy of religion, I would attempt to present the Christian concept of God. With this in mind I tried to express the idea that to Christians God is thought of as the eternal being, the mind that created the universe; a being that is totally different, totally 'other' from man, who, nevertheless, has revealed his nature through the person of Christ.

The difficulty is that the divine revelation is only perceived by the eye of faith. As Christ said, 'Seeing they do not see, and hearing they do not hear.' The divine revelation cannot be indisputably demonstrated. There is no way of 'unveiling' God so that the whole of humanity would have to acknowledge his existence. It is faith, and faith alone, which perceives the revelation.

Faith, however, is not something we earn or achieve by reason. It is a gift which is given in the revelation. We might be drawn towards this revelation by the observation of a pure, noble or good person, but we do not see God. We may see the activity of God in a person's life, but to see God's revelation requires the eye of faith. In short, we do not find God, but God finds us. Which comes first, faith or revelation? It is a chicken-and-egg question. When we are confronted by God, faith is born, or, if you like, when faith is born the revelation of God is seen.

This might sound like a contradiction of the idea of 'actively seeking God', because it is God who initiates our search. It is God who finds us, but it is still possible to turn away, to shade our eyes, to put up barriers, perhaps because at the back of our minds we are aware of the consequences of seeing the revelation of God. We know that our lives will inevitably be changed, and we don't want to change because we are comfortable as we are. 'Actively seeking God' means taking down the barriers we have built; once we do that, revelation is inevitable.

Sadly, many people manage to blindfold themselves to the divine revelation until they can no longer postpone the event. Deathbed conversions are not unusual, if only because at that time there is nowhere left to hide.

I thought it might be helpful if I were to share with George something of my own spiritual journey. I suggested that he attempt an experiment that I had tried once myself. It is nothing less than a deliberate removal of the blindfold, a decisive pulling down of the barriers, in so far as you are able. It is really an enactment of the prayer, 'Lord, I believe, help thou mine unbelief.' This was the experiment I conducted:

Each night before I lay down to sleep, I sat on my bed and said, 'God, if you exist, come into my life.' I must confess that I felt rather foolish at the time. I can now say, however, that Pascal was right: 'To seek God is to find him'; we discover that *we* have been found before we begin to look.

It is of course impossible to conjure up a mental image of God, but an image of Christ exists. God's revelation *is* Christ. Once we have opened our eyes to this fact we find ourselves on a spiritual helter skelter that hurls us into a universe that is limitless. The exciting thing is that the exploration begins here, not after death. To the Christian, God is love, and to explore God is to explore the heart of love. It is an exploration that will occupy us throughout eternity, but it starts here, in Norton Woodley, or wherever we might be.

If it sounds as if I delivered a monologue, then I'm afraid I did. I've had similar meetings in the past, and I'm aware that some people use their questions as a means of supporting their barriers. I was quite open about this and suggested that he saved his questions for the next time we met. I must say he was very thoughtful when he left; and we did arrange to meet again.

Well, I don't know if I did the right thing but I felt

that I didn't want to spend the afternoon playing metaphysical chess.

Best wishes,

Tommy

The Manse,
Nether Hadley

Dear Tommy,

It seems as if Norton Woodley is opening its doors to you, physically and spiritually. You are right about the clerical collar, but the collar itself does not win people. The collar may provide you with a superficial form of respect; it does not win people's love, only commitment to their needs and concerns, and a recognizable commitment to the love of God will do that.

It is important I think that you should be known to your community and not just to your church members. I don't mean that you should simply sport your clerical collar twice a week strolling up and down the High Street, though that alone would be a form of witness. It is a question of people knowing that you are easy to approach, available, accessible, that you care about people enough to give them more than just the time of day. You seem to be achieving this anyway, so keep up the good work.

You ask if you did the right thing with your solicitor friend. Who knows what is the right thing? No two people are alike. No two people have exactly the same needs. You have to obey your instinct and trust in God to do the rest. As you so rightly said, you will not reveal God to him. God will do that for himself. Only you can judge the mood of a person that you are talking to at a particular time. Don't worry too much about whether or not you have said the right thing. The important thing is that you did not run away from the situation. You did not make excuses, or palm him off with a book instead of a meeting.

Very often lay people tell me that they do not feel equipped to defend their beliefs out in the wicked world. It is hard for them to accept that they do not need to defend them, they need only to state them when asked, no matter how simply. I think that the unadorned witness of an ordinary Christian is probably far more helpful and effective than all our professional jargon. For example, I wouldn't be at all surprised if the principal things remembered by your solicitor are Sally's statement that when she worships and prays, her life works better than when she doesn't, and your challenge for him to invite God into his life. Nevertheless, I am sure he will have appreciated your earnest attempt to present the Christian view of God.

I wonder if I could set you a little exercise? You

mentioned Christ's words, 'Seeing they do not see, and hearing they do not hear.' Perhaps one of the most dramatic accounts of people having their eyes opened and seeing the revelation of God in Christ is the Emmaus road story. Study that passage, the gospel of Luke. Put yourself in the place of Cleopas. Imagine what thoughts passed through his mind at the moment of recognition, the moment of realization that sitting at his table was the risen Christ. Then perhaps the next time you see your solicitor you can study the passage together.

Keep me informed about John Fielding's progress.

God bless you,

Spoonbill

**The Manse,
Norton Woodley**

Dear Mr Spoonbill,

I have just spent an exhausting night. It is 8.30 a.m. and I have not been to bed, but I thought I would write to you in order to clarify my thoughts before I forget the details of what has happened.

At about 9.30 last night Mary Paine, Nicholas Paine's pretty wife, called at the manse. You may remember that Nicholas Paine is the Estate Manager at Woodley Grange and Richard Grey's right hand man. Well, Mary Paine practically fell through my door last night. She was very agitated. She said that a man called Benson-Hopwood was having a furious row with her husband and would I come at once and try to make them see sense. Within minutes I was climbing into her motorcar, foreign, very large and impressive with a tonneau boot, huge headlamps and a rather draughty canvas hood. On the way to Grange Gate she told me what had happened.

About once a month Nicholas Paine drives to Hereford for supplies that the local village stores do not stock. Apparently, he always calls at the Cloisters Hotel before returning to Woodley Vale. Benson-Hopwood apparently is a wholesale corn merchant in Hereford, and a friend had told him that his wife was in the habit of taking tea at the Cloisters and that her visits always happened to coincide with the visits of the Woodley Grange estate manager. Acting on this information Benson-Hopwood had marched round to the Cloisters just in time to see an impressive foreign motorcar driving away with his wife in the passenger seat.

When we arrived at Grange Gate, it was about 10.15. I could hear the two men shouting at each other, they sounded very angry and aggressive. It was really rather worrying. I wasn't quite sure what I was doing there.

When Mary Paine showed me into the study, the shouting stopped abruptly. Nicholas Paine, his chin thrust forward, his military moustache positively bristling, looked at me in amazement. 'Good God, Padre! What are you doing here?' Before I could answer, Mary Paine said, 'I asked him here because you two will listen to neither me nor each other. I thought Mr Sefton-Waters might restore a little sanity!' Both men looked shocked. Paine said, almost unbelievingly, 'You called in a parson! Are you out of your mind? This is a private matter. Do you think that. . . .' At that point I interrupted, I reminded him that priests and ministers had gone to the gallows rather than break their trust. I knew that apart from Mrs Paine's request the matter had absolutely nothing to do with me, but if I could help in any way I would; if not, I would leave and as far as I was concerned that would be the end of that.

Somehow my presence did seem to have a calming effect. Paine apologized to me, adding that he was also sorry that I had been 'dragged into this damned silly affair!' Benson-Hopwood said that he'd welcome an outsider's view; then perhaps Paine would see reason. Before Paine could respond to Benson-Hopwood I quickly outlined the problem from what little I knew. It was clear that Benson-Hopwood suspected that there was more to his wife's meetings with Nicholas Paine than tea and muffins.

Paine denied that he was up to anything unworthy. He claimed that he knew Mrs Benson-Hopwood from years ago because she had been at school with his sister. They'd met at the hotel about three months ago and simply had a chat, which he then told his wife about.

He had let Mrs Benson-Hopwood know that he came into Hereford on the first Friday of every month and she'd said, 'Oh good, I'll look forward to that.' Since that meeting they'd met twice and there was nothing more to it than that. When Benson-Hopwood had seen the two of them in the car, Paine insisted that he was simply dropping Mrs Benson-Hopwood off at her house on the Ludlow Road.

I asked Mr Benson-Hopwood what his wife had said about his suspicions. He said, 'When I spoke to her she just laughed and said "Wouldn't you like to know?" I could see I would get very little sense out of her. That's why I decided to have it out with Paine.' Then quite suddenly Benson-Hopwood said, 'Look here Paine, I've made a bit of a fool of myself. I think I'd better go.' He apologized to Mrs Paine, quite profusely. Finally he turned to me and offered to drop me off at Norton Woodley on his way back to Hereford. Mr and Mrs Paine looked extremely relieved. I think they're very close though there could be a problem there. Benson-Hopwood went out to his car whilst Mary Paine thanked me for helping.

On the way back to Norton Woodley we hardly spoke. When we arrived Benson-Hopwood switched off the engine and said, 'I know it's late, but do you think I could have a chat with you?' I invited him into the manse and offered him a drink. I said that I was afraid the best I could offer was either tea or perhaps a mug of cocoa. He laughed and said, 'Cocoa? I haven't had cocoa since I was at school.' The idea seemed to amuse him and yet at the same time appeal to him.

'Yes', he said. 'Why not?' Mrs McBride had left a fire set in the study, so I put a match to it and went out to make the cocoa.

He talked for a long time, well into the small hours of the morning. He was a successful business man but things were getting difficult for him because of the depression. Somewhere along the way his marriage had gone wrong. He didn't say so in as many words, but by implication I gathered that his wife drank rather heavily. They had one son, Martin, who was serving abroad in the army. Up to this point his conversation had been rational and normal, a little dispirited perhaps, but quite sane. He had just lit a cigar with the last match of the box, and he threw the empty matchbox into the fire. It flared briefly and he stared at the embers as if transfixed. I think it was from that moment that he began to lose control. I didn't notice it immediately. He began to complain about his employees. He said there were thieves among them. Eventually he was saying that they were all thieves and scoundrels and that his wife had arranged this to ruin him.

He started walking about the room throwing small objects for me to catch. I had to stop him as the objects got bigger. I rushed over to him when he laid his hands on a very large concordance with apparently every intention of throwing the book at me. Then I noticed that not only were his accusations getting wilder, but he seemed to be talking in rhyming couplets. It was reasonably logical, given that what he was saying was outrageous anyway, but everything he said seemed to rhyme. 'I'll get to the bottom of their rotten affairs and then I'll kick them down the stairs.' 'Just you wait and then you'll see, try as they might, they won't beat me.' I was completely nonplussed. He seemed to have gone off his head and yet was maintaining a strange sort of logic. At about 5.30 a.m. he said, 'Tired, very tired.' I helped him onto the sofa and in no time he was asleep. I crept out into the hallway and telephoned Dr Langton. About half an hour later the doctor arrived; Benson-Hopwood woke and Langton gave him some kind of sleeping tablet. I explained to the doctor what had happened since our arrival at the manse, saying that Benson-Hopwood had been distressed earlier in the evening but that I couldn't go into the details about that. An ambulance arrived shortly afterwards and the doctor and his patient departed.

Dawn had broken and the sun was well into the new day. It was a beautiful morning. There was that wonderfully fresh, clean feeling in the air. I was exhausted. Yet I knew that I wouldn't be able to sleep until I'd walked a little.

As I reached the bridge who should be crossing but Iris Gumley, goodness knows where she was going at that hour. When she saw me she said, 'Having a nice morning stroll?' I just smiled and then to my amazement she sniffed and said, 'Well, it's all right for those who 'aven't any work to do.' I didn't know whether to laugh or cry.

I realize now that I can't go to bed immediately. I promised to visit a young mother to make arrangements for the baptism of her child. Ah well, I'm glad I've written to you before I slept, otherwise I might have woken up thinking I'd had a bad dream. What a night!

Yours ever,

Tommy

The Manse,
Nether Hadley

Dear Old Warrior,

What a night! Indeed!

You were saying, not so long ago, that whatever else can be said about village life, it was never boring for a parson. I think I can safely say that the work of a minister is never boring *wherever* he may be.

Few people realize just how much of the pastoral work of a minister belongs to an entirely secret world which, by its very nature, must always remain strictly confidential. There will be, over the years, so many conversations, arguments, rages, tears, so many moments of high drama that will have to be locked away in the vaults of your mind. Many people find it difficult to imagine what a minister finds to do between Sundays. You will have to suffer many jokes about working 'one day a week'.

Very often we are accused of being 'out of touch' with the real world. As you know, nothing could be further from the truth. Most people's lives are confined to a particular line of work, their days spent in an office, or a factory, or a shop or a farm. They may read in the newspapers about death, divorce and disaster, and discuss these events avidly with their friends and colleagues, and feel that they are in touch with the *real* world. It is the minister who holds the hands of the dying, comforts the bereaved, stands beside those whose marriages are in distress, not once, but time and time again. He is involved in more crises in a year than most people experience in a lifetime.

But the calling of a minister is a life-long commitment to service. You are Christ's servant, and therefore the servant of all. If you can remind yourself of this daily you will avoid the temptation of thinking that the minister is 'somebody' in the community.

The temptations are all about you. You stand in a pulpit, high and lifted up, you preach and teach, you chair meetings, you celebrate the sacraments. It is all too easy for self-importance to take root.

The fact that you have intimate knowledge of the private lives of so many people can give you a false sense of power. Knowledge is a powerful weapon that we must never abuse. We are servants. The knowledge we gain is not our personal possession. We are servants of Christ, entrusted with confessions that are made to God not to us. Everything we have and are belongs to him. We offer ourselves to be used as instruments of the Holy Spirit. If we are used, that is a privilege and not an achievement.

I am saying all this to you, because in recent months you have been thrown headlong into some of the more onerous responsibilities of the ministry. You must never 'count your successes', they are not yours. All you can do is thank God for the opportunities of service, and trust that you will be fit to continue in his service.

It is interesting to consider the word 'real'. The dictionary defines 'real' as 'actually existing or occurring; objective; genuine; consisting of immovable property such as land or houses.'

'Immovable property'? There are grassy mounds where castles once stood, deserts where crops once grew, mountains that have tumbled, towns and villages that have disappeared beneath the sea or in the path of volcanic eruption. Certainly the things men have made must count among the most insubstantial. To the Christian the only realities are the things of the spirit. Love, hope and courage, these things never die, yet people worry about their clothes, their appearance, their status in the community, such fleeting, trivial things. All these things surround the self, 'me' and 'mine' and 'I' exist in the centre of life and the world revolves around 'me and mine'!

Remember, a stumbling block to faith for many people is the idea that in order truly to live, we have to die to self, and in dying to self we find real life. This is true for the minister as it is for anybody else. So do remember that when the secrets of people's hearts and minds are entrusted to you, they are not your secrets, they are not your people. If you truly die to yourself and in so doing give the Holy Spirit room to work through you, then you will find that you are truly alive, perhaps you will experience the joy of the reality of the presence of God.

Tommy, I was full of sympathy for you after your dreadful night, but I could not help smiling when you said that you couldn't go to bed until you had arranged a baptism. It is somehow wonderfully ironic that from the incredibly entangled complexities of adult life you were thrown immediately into contact with the innocence of a child.

You know Christ's saying, 'unless you become as a little child, you shall in no wise enter the kingdom of heaven'. Well, I once had an aunt, Aunt Emily, who was considered by many to be childlike. Everything excited her; everything seemed to delight her. She was forever drawing our attention to a bird or a tree, or a flower, or distant hill, or a pattern on a table-cloth. Her conversation was punctuated by 'ooohs' and 'aaahs'. She could make an adventure out of a walk down the garden or opening a packet of tea. Children loved her of course, because she could enter their world so easily. It is only adults who find that days and years go so quickly. An hour in the garden can be a complete life-time, an eternity to a child, and to my Aunt Emily.

To see the world with the eyes of a child is to see everything new. That is what is so exciting about the baptism of a child. In baptism we see new life, new hope, new promise. The sacrament declares the prevenient love of God, that is the recognition that God loves us before we either understand, or are able to respond to his love. It is the outward sign of God's love anticipating our need for his love. Baptism tells us that God's love is the foundation of life in Christ, that ultimately we love God because he first loved us. It is the outward welcoming into the fellowship of the body of Christ. In a sense baptism means a new existence, a new birth, to be born with Christ and to live a risen life with him.

There are those who do not believe in infant baptism, saying that you should choose to be baptized when you are old enough to decide that you want to become a Christian. To use this is a complete misunderstanding of baptism as a God-given means of grace. The whole point of baptism is that it is the sacrament that celebrates the unmerited gift of God's grace and love. We can never earn God's love or even choose to have it. Baptism is a declaration that God loves us regardless of whether or not we know or deserve it. The lavish generosity of God's love does not depend on human qualifications. To have to qualify for baptism reduces the sacrament to a mere initiation rite.

Innocence faces many attacks over the years. We are taught to be independent, to be self-assured, to think for ourselves. In time innocence becomes mere naïvety. Sadly, worldly wisdom makes heaven more distant because we find it difficult to accept the grace and love of God. We learn to 'achieve', to 'earn', we become cynical of anything that is given freely. We learn materialistic aphorisms such as 'You get nothing for nothing', or 'You only get what you pay for'.

When you baptize this infant be aware of the child's total dependence on others. Watch small children at play and you will see unself-conscious joy and receptive faces. Babies do not earn love or achieve happiness, they simply accept what is given them. To a child, the gates of heaven are not forced open by righteous deeds or pious determination, they open by grace.

It is a great privilege to baptize a child, for if in seeing the child's helplessness we are able to accept, like a child, the love we have not earned, in that moment we enjoy the peace that passes understanding.

In many ways I have been privileged to officiate in your three-year baptism into the ministry, I have seen the grace of God being poured out from you and I have shared in the joy of it. Take a tip from my Aunt Emily, Thomas, never get used to anything. Never grow 'old and wise', remember always that you are a child of God, and the thrill of life, the excitement of discovery and the wonder of the magnitude of God's love will enable you to start each day with the joy of those who have become as children in the heavenly Kingdom.

God bless you Thomas,

Spoonbill

Dear Mr Spoonbill,

Just a quick note. Today was the day of the baptism. John Fielding was in the congregation. The child howled almost continually whilst I held her, but it was still a beautiful service. The crowning joy for me was that through the child's heart-rending shrieks I caught a sight of John Fielding. For the first time in my three years at Norton Woodley I saw him smile.

Wonders never cease, do they?
Yours ever,

Tommy

P.S. As an encore for joy, when I got back to the manse, there was a cottage loaf in the porch with a note. It said, 'God bless you – Mrs Driver.' He does, doesn't he?

Index